French Legends: The Life and Legacy of Marie Antoinette

By Charles River Editors

Marie Antoinette by Joseph Ducreux

About Charles River Editors

Charles River Editors was founded by Harvard and MIT alumni to provide superior editing and original writing services, with the expertise to create digital content for publishers across a vast range of subject matter. In addition to providing original digital content for third party publishers, Charles River Editors republishes civilization's greatest literary works, bringing them to a new generation via ebooks.

Visit charlesrivereditors.com for more information.

Introduction

Marie Antoinette (1755-1793)

Painting: *Maria Antonia playing the clavichord*, **Franz Xaver Wagenschön (1769)**

"I was a queen, and you took away my crown; a wife, and you killed my husband; a mother, and you deprived me of my children. My blood alone remains: take it, but do not make me suffer long." – Marie Antoinette

A lot of ink has been spilled covering the lives of history's most influential figures, but how much of the forest is lost for the trees? In Charles River Editors' French series, readers can get caught up to speed on the lives of France's most important men and women in the time it takes to finish a commute, while learning interesting facts long forgotten or never known.

Throughout history, a countless numer of historical figures have had their lives overshadowed by the myths and legends that surround them to the extent that their legacy comes to define them. In French history, this is truer of Marie Antoinette than just about everyone else. Nearly 220 years after she was put to the guillotine, Marie Antoinette is more famous than ever, fairly or unfairly coming to epitomize royalty and everything that was wrong with it.

As the youngest daughter of the Holy Roman Emperor, 14 year old Marie's marriage to the eventual Louis XVI made her Dauphine, and it initially seemed like a good fit. The charming and beautiful young girl pleased the French, but she had the misfortune of being queen at a time when the French were beginning to sour on their royalty and aristocratic classes. On top of that, France's participation in the American Revolution had left the nation broke, which only angered those who watched the King and Queen spend millions of livres for their own comfort at the expense of the state. Though Marie Antoinette was hardly the only French royal who liked to live lavishly, the French were particularly scornful of her, possibly due to her Austrian ancestry.

As France slid toward its own Revolution, rumors and innuendo against the queen took hold, and she was accused of being promiscuous and even defrauding a jeweler in what became known as the "Diamond Necklace Affair". Though the rumors had no basis in truth, they were widely accepted and eventually used as partial justification for her execution. By 1792, with the Revolution in full swing, the Royal Family's attempt to escape Paris was thwarted, and in January 1793, Louis XVI lost his head at the hands of the Jacobins. With her own health failing, the Queen herself was tried the following October, accused of sexually abusing the sickly Dauphin. Given that she had spent the last few years of her life carefully doting on her children at the expense of almost everything else, it was a particularly heinous accusation. On October 16, 1793, Antoinette herself was executed at the guillotine.

Since her death, Marie Antoinette has been the subject of sharp historical debate over whether she was actually a catalyst in the French Revolution or simply an insignificant scapegoat who was unfairly made a target. At the same time, the one thing everybody associates with Antoinette is the phrase "Let them eat cake", a spoiled and ignorant comment supposedly made in response to being informed that the peasants had no bread. While that phrase has been used far and wide to depict someone as being out of touch, there's no indication Antoinette ever said anything like it. Nevertheless, she remains a pop culture fixture across the West, perceived just as negatively in death as she was in life.

French Legends: The Life and Legacy of Marie Antoinette looks at the life of the famous French Queen, attempting to separate fact from fiction and analyzing her legacy. Along with pictures of important people, places, and events, you will learn about Marie Antoinette like you never have before, in no time at all.

Marie Antoinette at age 13 by Martin van Meytens, 1767

Chapter 1: Her Royal Highness Archduchess Maria Antonia of Austria, 1755-1770

Maria Antonia Josepha Joanna was born on November 2, 1755, the 15th and final child born to the Holy Roman Emperor Francis I. Though the world would come to know her as Marie Antoinette, she was called Antonia and Madame Antoine as a girl, and she was described as "a small, but completely healthy Archduchess". Her mother, the Holy Roman Empress Maria Theresa was so accustomed to giving birth by then that she worked on imperial paperwork throughout her labor. In fact, Maria Theresa labored and birthed privately, unlike her daughter many years later.

The fact that Maria Theresa had so many children is made all the more remarkable by the fact that she was actually the power behind the throne. A 1713 law in Austria-Hungary had allowed for female succession, and Maria Theresa was crowned in 1740. Thus, Marie Antoinette's father, Francis Stephen, Duke of Lorraine, held no power in the royal court. The two were happily married, as their union was a rare love match, and Maria Theresa bore sixteen children during their marriage, ten of whom lived to adulthood.

Maria Theresa

These sixteen children can be divided into two groups, separated by approximately five years due to the death of a sibling. While Maria Theresa encouraged her daughters to grow up to be obedient wives, she herself said that she would have ridden into battle, if only she wasn't pregnant. Marie Antoinette was the fifteenth child born to the Empress, with even her multi-lingual name, Antoine, speaking to the expectation that she would leave to make a diplomatic marriage. Antoine's close siblings included Maria Carolina, called Charlotte, Ferdinand, and Maximilian. All were born within a period of approximately three years. Franz Stephen died in 1765, and Marie Antoinette's oldest brother, Joseph II was later crowned Emperor of the Holy Roman Empire, ruling alongside his mother.

Raised at the Hofberg and Schonbrunn Palaces in Vienna, as well as a smaller country palace in Laxenburg, Marie Antoinette had a happy childhood. Her parents maintained a casual and relaxed court, with relatively few formal restrictions upon behavior or associations, and Francis I enjoyed spending time with his children, creating a much closer family life than was typical for eighteenth-century royalty. With so many young children, the family itself provided plenty of close sibling relationships, especially between Marie and sister Charlotte.

Barring court appearances, the children were allowed a childhood not so different from those in the upper middle class, including relatively casual dress. Summers at the Schonbrunn Palace included time in the gardens and menagerie, often open to the public allowing the royal family to interact with their subjects. The young Archdukes and Archduchesses were not only allowed, but encouraged to make friends with common children. Both the Hofberg and Schonbrunn Palaces were in the city and quite accessible to the people. Parties and festivals made visits to the Laxenburg Palace, a refurbished hunting lodge, a favorite with the children, including Marie Antoinette.

While Maria Theresa devoted herself to ruling an empire, she did choose her children's governesses and tutors with some care. She, herself, paid relatively little attention to her children and was often harsh with all but her favorite, the Archduchess Marie Christine, thirteen years older than little Antoine. Antoine was closest to Maria Caroline, only three years older, during her childhood. The two looked very much alike and were educated alongside one another.

Like most princesses of her time, Marie Antoinette's education was largely focused on social and religious education, including music and dance. She enjoyed theater and performed for the court as a child, singing at her parents' name day celebrations when she was only four. In 1762, just before her sixth birthday, Marie Antoinette heard Mozart, himself a young child, play at court. The young girl herself learned to play the harpsichord, harp, spinet and clavichord, and given the multi-lingual environment of the royal court, it was no surprise she could sing French songs and Italian arias. Young Madame Antoine also excelled at dancing so much so that it caught the eye of several observers; British Whig Horace Walpole quoted Virgil to describe her, "She was in truth revealed to be a goddess by her step."

At the same time, Marie was expected to be a queen, so much of her time was spent on the social norms of being a perfect wife. Royal chaplains saw to her religious education, and she certainly learned her prayers during her girlhood. Like other noble girls of the time, Antoine was encouraged to practice needlepoint and embroidery. Casual and relaxed portraits of Marie-Antoinette as a girl with her family show not only the atmosphere of the Viennese court, but also her playing with dolls, perhaps foreshadowing her love of fashion. She was very fond of her dogs and liked horses, but was not taught to ride.

Marie depicted in hunting attire, by Joseph Krantzinger (1771)

Chapter 2: Her Royal Highness The Dauphine of France, 1770-1774

The Engagement

In many respects, Marie Antoinette did not have the typical royal childhood, especially in comparison to the isolated nature her future husband Louis XVI had growing up. But that unique childhood did not extend to all aspects of life.

When Madame Antoine was only eight years old, negotiations began concerning the young girl's marriage. Austria and France had allied themselves during the Seven-Years War, working together against Prussia, and when that war ended in 1763, discussions of a marital alliance began immediately. The alliance had already proven beneficial, and a marriage between the two royal houses would cement the alliance after the end of the Seven-Years War. The marriage was negotiated between Maria Theresa and the French King, Louis XV. While the aging Louis XV considered marrying an Austrian Archduchess himself, he decided the heir to the throne, Louis XVI, was a better prospect. In 1767, Maria Theresa had a number of marriageable daughters, ranging in age from 12 to 23 years old, but unfortunately smallpox took the life of one of the Archduchesses in 1767 and left another badly scarred. The three girls remaining included the Archduchesses Charlotte, Amalia and Antoine. Charlotte was to be married to the King of Naples and Amalia to Don Ferdinand of Parma. That left Antoine with Louis August, the grandson of Louis XV and Dauphin of France.

Louis Auguste as Dauphin of France, by Louis-Michel Van Loo (1769).

Ambassadors between France and Austria described the young girl as having a fair white complexion, blue eyes and a full lower lip. Her hair was thick and blonde and she was quite petite and slender, as court fashion required. She was criticized for her crooked teeth, and an oral surgeon was summoned from France to correct her smile, a painful process completed without anesthesia. The King of France, Louis XV, was especially concerned with the girl's appearance. Surviving letters reveal concerns about the size of her breasts, excused by Maria Theresa on the grounds of the girl's youth. At thirteen, she had not yet reached puberty. Portraits were sent to the French, but Maria Theresa was displeased with their quality.

Following her engagement, Marie Antoinette spent the remaining years of her childhood preparing for her future role. She practiced French with French actors from the theater and also Abbe Vermond, a priest sent by Louis XV to the Austrian court. Abbe Vermond found the young princess to have an excellent character and heart, but he thought she was rather poorly educated. She struggled with reading and writing, even in her native German. Abbe Vermond said she was more intelligent than was said, and worked to improve her French, her reading and writing and to teach French history. She was particularly fond of French history and genealogy, much to Vermond's pleasure. Her dance master saw to it that she practiced walking in the elaborate court dress and high-heeled shoes worn at Versailles so she could glide through the dirty halls of Versailles with grace. Maria Theresa herself taught Marie Antoinette to play cards, hoping to reduce the potential for costly gambling debts. Gambling was favored at all the courts of Europe, including Vienna.

Maria Theresa ordered a huge wardrobe for Marie Antoinette's bridal trousseau, turning the relaxed young Austrian princess into a French dauphine. These jeweled dresses, petticoats, undergarments and slippers cost the Habsburg Empire some 400,000 livres. In modern terms, a livre is approximately $20-30, making clear just how extravagant the wardrobe was. Her entire wardrobe was sewn from French fabrics by French tailors and seamstresses, and a formal gilded, glass-sided carriage was built for the young girl's journey to France. The young girl would also be provided with a generous dowry. After much negotiation, it was decided that the girl would make the official transfer from Austria to France on a deserted island on the Rhine River. When Maria Theresa consulted an astrologer about her daughter's fate, he responded, ominously, "There are crosses for all shoulders".

MARIE ANTOINNETTE   ARCHIDUCHESSE
SOEUR DE   L'EMPERUER
DAUPHINE   DE FRANCE·
NÉE A VIENNE   LE 2 Nov.bre 1755·

DU SANG LE PLUS AUGUSTE ELLE A REÇU LE JOUR
ET SON MOINDRE MERITE EST SA HAUTE NAISSANCE
MINERVE AVEC TENDRESSE ELEVA SON ENFANCE
ELLE EN FIT L'ORNEMENT D'UNE BRILLANTE COUR
AUJOURD'HUI TOUS LES DIEUX INSPIRES PAR L'AMOUR
COMBLENT PAR SON HYMEN LE BONHEUR DE LA FRANCE

Profile medallion of Marie Antoinette as Dauphine of France in 1770,

The Journey

On April 19, 1770, Marie Antoinette and Louis XV were married by proxy, a wedding tradition that was traditionally performed before a princess was taken to her new home. Marie Antoinette's brother Ferdinand stood in for the French dauphin in the Augustine Church in Vienna. Two days later, on April 21, 1770, Marie Antoinette bade goodbye to her family and home, undertaking a two-week journey to France. The princess' entourage included 57 carriages, 117 footmen, and 376 horses. Thousands of relief horses were placed along her route. The people came out to watch the princess pass, revealed by the glass-sided carriage.

Upon reaching the island, the young princess was stripped naked in a room full of French courtiers. All of her Austrian possessions and connections, from her ladies-in-waiting to her pug, Mops, were taken from her. The courtiers present criticized her body, adding to the modest girl's discomfort. While formal toilette and dressing rituals were common in the French court, the Austrian princess had always been allowed some degree of modesty and privacy at home. New French garments, from her underthings to her gown, replaced those she had worn. She was able to keep only a small watch from her mother. She cried as she bade goodbye to her ladies and attendants.

Following this ritual transition from Austria to France, the young girl met King Louis XV and the dauphin Louis XVI in Compeigne, approximately 50 miles northeast of Paris. Louis XV was impressed by the dauphine, calling her pretty, but somewhat child-like. Upon their first meeting, Marie Antoinette forgot court etiquette and ran up to the king, curtseying, but he was charmed by the breach of etiquette, and Marie Antoinette and Louis XV remained close throughout the remainder of the king's life.

Louis XV, by Maurice Quentin de La Tour, (1748)

The French people, already struggling with the costs of the Seven-Years War, welcomed the new Dauphine of France, who was greeted with shouts and cheers wherever she went. Initially, her welcome to France was quite warm. The pretty young girl held the promise of succession to the throne and she smiled and greeted her new subjects. At the same time, some courtiers were nervous about the tense relationship between France and Austria, which had traditionally been antagonistic and had only recently improved during the Seven-Years War. To these courtiers, the new Dauphine represented a potentially foreign threat who might prove more loyal to Austria than France.

Inadvertently, the Dauphine was helped by the fact the Dauphin seemed the exact opposite of her. In comparison to the petite and pretty young girl, Louis XVI was an awkward, introverted and shy boy of 15. He was also prone to being heavy and considered generally unattractive. Moreover, Louis XVI was relatively uninterested in the young princess, preferring hunting and spending time in the smithy he had built at Versailles. An intelligent young man, he enjoyed reading and had an interest in the philosophy of the day, including the work of David Hume. He took great pleasure in his meals, eating large quantities, but did not enjoy balls, dancing or games.

Wedding Night

Marie Antoinette and Louis XVI married officially on May 16, 1770 in the royal chapel at Versailles, and royal custom required that the couple be publicly bedded. When the wedding feast ended, the newlyweds were led to their marriage bed by the king. A priest blessed the wedding bed and courtiers surrounded the couple as they were undressed before everyone and re-dressed in finely made nightgowns. Both climbed into bed and the curtains were closed and opened again so the courtiers could say goodnight. The young couple was finally alone.

In the morning, the news soon spread that the sheets were unmarred by blood and the princess was still a virgin. Rumors began to fly immediately regarding the Dauphine's temperament or willingness in the marital bed. Though any lack of marital consummation was almost certainly not her fault, the young Dauphine was blamed for the failure to consummate the marriage and conceive an heir to the throne. The two eventually grew closer and the Dauphin began to show affection to Marie Antoinette, but he still refused to share her bed.

Maria Theresa wrote her daughter, concerned about the status of the marriage. She encouraged her to be gentle and sweet and cajole the Dauphin with caresses. While Marie Antoinette was certainly concerned about the state of her relationship and need for an heir, she was not successful in her attempts to encourage the Dauphin to consummate their marriage. She took up riding and hunting in an attempt to bond with her husband and read history to provide subjects for the two to discuss. While Maria Theresa criticized Antoinette for riding, particularly riding astride, the young Dauphine defended her actions. During these years, the Dauphin's younger brother, the Comte de Provence married. There was great concern that the new Comtesse would become pregnant before Antoinette. The Comte de Provence was, however, also unable to consummate his marriage.

Life at Versailles

Château de Versailles as seen from the Place d'Armes, 1722, Pierre-Denis Martin.

The Palace of Versailles was nothing like the Hofburg or Schonbrunn Palaces in Vienna. The grand palace, built by Louis XIV, the Sun King, was made up of grand chambers, gilded walls and formal gardens. When the princess arrived, her own chambers were not complete and she was placed into an unused suite of rooms. The rooms were dusty, with cloths still covering the outdated furniture.

Today Versailles is viewed as Europe's most decadent and grand palace, and though the palace was obviously very grand in 1770, sanitation was poor. There was a strong odor of urine and feces in the palace, with both human and pet waste present in the halls. The first toilets were installed in 1768, but by 1789, there were only nine toilets in the palace. The palace was not only home to the royal family and staff, but more than 350 additional rooms and apartments, ranging from grand suites of rooms to single rooms. Some of the nobility lived in Versailles all the time, while others maintained townhouses nearby and used their rooms for dressing. Rank denoted the quality of accommodations at the palace. Depending upon the time of year, the population of the palace could number well into the thousands. And while the Viennese palaces were located near the people, Versailles was 12 miles outside of Paris and quite isolated from the French people.

The French court was also far more constraining than the one Madame Antoine grew up in. Formal, public court ritual was constant, from the time the Dauphine rose in the morning until she went to bed at night. Her retinue was substantial, and the rank of the ladies present was a constant concern, from the lowest members of her household to the three daughters of Louis XV, the princesses of the blood royal. The Comtesse de Noailles ran the young girl's household and served as her primary instructor in court etiquette. The noblest tasks, those requiring the most contact with the Dauphine herself, had to be assigned to the highest ranking individual present, so if someone new should enter, the ritual had to begin again. In many cases, the morning toilette left the dauphine undressed, shivering, while the routine began again and again for her to put on the layers required by court dress. The full practice took several hours, including hairstyling, applying rouge, dressing and powdering her towering hairstyle.

The Dauphine was expected to visit the three unmarried princesses, Adelaide, Sophie and Victoire daily. The three were not fond of the young princess or the Austrian alliance, but they were one of her few social contacts in her first days at Versailles and the young Louis was quite fond of them. Madame Adelaide had already dubbed the girl "l'Autricienne", meaning the Austrian. Unfortunately, the term also combines the words autruche ("ostrich") and chienne ("bitch"), which subsequently provided the ideal inspiration for unfortunate cartoons and satire in later years. The royal aunts took advantage of Marie Antoinette's innocence, turning her strongly against the King's mistress, Madame du Barry. The young Dauphine refused to speak to Madame du Barry, even at the King's request. She continued in her refusal until New Year's Day, 1772, when she finally relented and made a comment to Madame du Barry. While angered by this, she began showing slightly more tolerance for the King's mistress, to his great pleasure.

While Louis Auguste did not dance, he and the Dauphine hosted and attended dances together, as well as hunting, playing cards and playing billiards. The Comte and Comtesse de Provence often joined them. At one of these dances, she and the Princesse de Lamballe, a wealthy young widow, became friends. As a descendant of Louis XIV, she was of an acceptable social status to befriend the Dauphine, and their close friendship would continue for many years to come. The young Princesse de Lamballe had an excellent reputation and did not involve herself in court intrigue.

Princesse de Lamballe

Between 1770 and 1774, the Dauphine began to throw more elaborate parties and started attending the opera regularly in Paris. Her visits were welcomed in the city and she took great delight in the theater, just as she had as a child. She also promoted her favorites, including Christoph Willibald Gluck.

Not surprisingly, the Dauphine's expenses grew substantially during these years. The parties and masked balls, as well as gambling debts, were costly. While those costs were widely accepted as the cost of doing business for royals, the Dauphine far exceeded her annual clothing allowance, ordering a multitude of new gowns, shoes, gloves and adornments. While her spending was certainly quite high, her gowns and accessories were often given to her ladies as payment after they were worn.

Antoinette in an extravagant court dress

Chapter 3: Her Majesty The Queen of France and Navarre, 1774-1791

On April 27, 1774, while on a hunting trip, King Louis XV fell ill. After he returned to Versailles, the cause of his illness was clear by early May. Pustules had appeared and the aging King realized that he had smallpox. King Louis XV sent Madame du Barry away before he made his final confession for the sake of his soul. A candle in the window of the royal chamber burned as long as the King lived. On May 10, 1774, the candle in his chamber was extinguished, announcing his death.

Louis XVI and Marie Antoinette were greeted, first by the Comtesse de Noailles, then by other nobles as the King and Queen of France, but matters were hardly ceremonious. Everyone fled Versailles to avoid the risk of contagion that afternoon, and they would not return to Versailles for six months. Marie Antoinette, having had smallpox as a young child, was not at risk, but the King was. King Louis XV was interred with great haste to prevent the spread of the disease.

The newly crowned couple brought great hope to the troubled country, which had initially favored Louis XV but came to dislike him as his later reign damaged French standing and its treasury. Many historians would later attribute the French Revolution to Louis XV, not his better known and ill-fated grandson. Louis XVI was only the second French king crowned in the 18th century, and though Louis XV had tarnished the notion of absolute monarchy to a great extent, the French people still saw in the new king and queen the potential of a stable and responsible royal couple.

While French queens traditionally held little power under Salic law, Marie Antoinette was well-liked and well-regarded. Even lacking royal power, the queen did wield substantial financial power, particularly given that Louis XVI at this time had no interest in other women and did not have a mistress. She was encouraged to look after Austrian interests by her friend and confidant, Florimund Mercy, Comte d'Argenteau, who was now one of the most visible and influential members of the royal court. Mercy, an Austrian minister, also provided Maria Theresa and later the Emperor Joseph with detailed information on Marie Antoinette's activities.

Comte de Mercy-Argenteau

Marie Antoinette's social circle grew in the years after 1774 as she gradually befriended a small circle of young women, many of whom were less respectable than the Princesse de Lamballe.

One of her new acquaintances was the Comtesse de Polignac, who was considered good-humored and soon ingratiated herself and her family with the young queen. Comtesse de Polignac would parlay this favorable standing into being assigned the position of governess to the royal children. While the Princesse de Lamballe would eventually be given the title Superintendent of the Household, Marie Antoinette's fondness for her began to fade in later years.

While Louis XVI's coronation was planned for 1775, there were no plans to crown Marie Antoinette Queen of France. While the Controller General of Finance, Anne Robert Turgot, recommended a small Parisian coronation, Louis planned a grand affair, complete with a new suit of clothes and crown, as well as a lavish gown for Marie Antoinette. However, the crown's finances were not good and a poor harvest compounded the financial challenges in France. In early May, riots, called the Flour Wars, broke out among the peasantry. While Marie Antoinette is not often remembered for her kindness and compassion, in a letter to Maria Theresa, she expressed concern and sadness for the people of France. That same year, the young queen rescued an orphaned boy nearly trampled beneath her carriage, bringing him to Versailles and seeing to his education.

Marie Antoinette, Queen of France, in coronation robes by Jean-Baptiste Gautier Dagoty, 1775.

At the suggestion of the Comte Noailles, the King gave Marie Antoinette her own residence on the grounds of Versailles, the Petit Trianon. There, the Queen created a simple and personal retreat surrounded by gardens. Eventually, the complex expanded to include a created village, complete with a dairy, well-groomed cows and chickens, and this pretense of the simple farm life was supported by nearby farms that provided fresh fruits and vegetables. The Queen and her ladies gave up formal court dress at the Petit Trianon in favor of simple cotton muslin gowns with a drawstring neck and plain sash. While her choice was not political, cotton was an imported fabric, while the silk of court dresses was produced in France. Libelles distributed in

Paris implied that the simple muslin dresses worn at the Petit Trianon allowed for easy sexual access. Moreover, even though her residence and redesigning of the Petit Trianon was intended to be a way of demonstrating the ability to live more simply and cheaply, the Queen would eventually be criticized for the splendor surrounding the home, and rumors spread that she had adorned the inside with gold.

The Queen in a "muslin" dress, Élisabeth Vigée-Lebrun (1783). The portrait was criticized by many as not befitting a queen.

Petit Trianon

While traditionally life at the French court had been purely public, at the Petit Trianon, she could have privacy. Marie Antoinette spent a significant amount of time at the Petit Trianon, even spending nights there away from the court. She invited her closest friends to join her, as well as the King on occasion. Among the friends who joined Marie Antoinette at the Petit Trianon was Swedish Count Axel von Fersen the Younger. Marie Antoinette and Count von Fersen were clearly close, but the nature of their relationship is unclear. Rumors have persisted that they may have had a sexual relationship, but given that the Queen was rarely alone, it would've been difficult for her to have an extramarital affair. Nevertheless, rumors questioned the paternity of the Queen's children, but the King did not, and recent biographers note that the young Louis-Charles was said to have resembled other relatives of Louis XVI, further discrediting the notion that he was Fersen's son.

Count Axel von Fersen

Sexuality and Motherhood

In August 1775, the Comtesse d'Artois, wife of Louis' youngest brother, the Comte d'Artois, gave birth to a healthy baby boy, the first Bourbon prince of their generation. Louis and Marie Antoinette had already been married for more than five years. By the late fall, the Comtesse d'Artois was expecting again.

The fall of 1775 saw the publication of a pamphlet, called Les Nouvelles de la Cour. This graphic pamphlet or libelle dissected the royal couple's sexual relationship or lack thereof in obscene detail. It suggested a lesbian relationship between the Princesse de Lamballe and the Queen, and the author went on to imply that Maria Theresa had even suggested the Queen take a lover to secure an heir. While gentlemen in the court may have expressed interest in an illicit relationship with Marie Antoinette, she remained chaste. In fact, her modesty was referred to by one of her ladies as "extreme".

Several suggestions have been made regarding physical difficulties, including the possibility of phimosis. There is no evidence that the Dauphin had a surgical procedure to correct any physical defect, and when examined by a physician on the king's orders, he was found to be "well made". Furthermore, the Dauphin's own diaries do not suggest any break in hunting activities, which would have been required if he had been circumcised to correct phimosis. While the frank discussion with the physician improved relations between the two and encouraged intimacy, the marriage was still not fully consummated.

Finally, after many letters, Maria Theresa sent Emperor Joseph II to France in April 1777 to assess and correct the problem between the two. Joseph spoke with both Marie Antoinette and Louis XVI about their relationship. He wrote to his mother regarding the difficulties between the two, explaining that the Dauphin could sustain an erection, but did not ejaculate during attempts at intercourse. In a letter to his brother, Joseph called the two "complete blunderers," blaming both the King and his sister's lack of sexual appetite. Seven years after the wedding, Marie Antoinette wrote to her mother that their marriage was finally consummated and she could hope for a pregnancy. Both Marie Antoinette and Louis XVI wrote to Joseph to thank him for his intervention in the months following.

On December 19, 1778, the long-awaited first child of the king, a girl named Marie-Therese Charlotte, arrived. As was becoming in vogue at the time, the Queen tried to breastfeed the newborn princess. The birth of the Dauphin, Louis Joseph, followed in 1781. Louis Charles, the royal couple's second son, was born in 1785, and many critics noted that Louis-Charles was born almost exactly 9 months after Count Fersen had visited the Queen. A fourth child, a daughter named Sophie Beatrix, was born, possibly prematurely, in 1786, but lived less than a year.

Marie Antoinette had some difficulties with the birth of her first child and her health suffered significantly after the birth of Sophie. Furthermore, the Dauphin was a sickly child and died in 1789 of spinal tuberculosis. However, Marie Antoinette was a devoted mother, spending as much time as possible with her children and seeing to their education. And regardless of rumors concerning the Queen's infidelity, the King clearly continued to visit her bedroom.

The Queen with Marie-Therese and the Dauphin

The Diamond Necklace Affair

While the birth of several royal children secured the succession, Marie Antoinette had decidedly fallen out of favor. A 1785 scandal, typically called the diamond necklace affair, illustrates just how far she had fallen. The Queen was not involved or implicated in the scandal, but she was, nonetheless, held responsible by the people and the illicit press.

In 1772, King Louis XV ordered a grand diamond necklace made for his mistress, Madame du Barry, by the jewelers Boehmer and Bassenge. The King died before the necklace was finished, so the Queen was offered the opportunity to purchase the necklace in 1778 and again in 1781, but refused.

A con artist in the court, Jeanne de la Motte, saw an opportunity, along with her husband and several conspirators. She was the mistress of the Cardinal de Rohan, who had been the French ambassador to the court in Vienna but had fallen out of favor with the Queen. Jeanne de la Motte convinced the Cardinal de Rohan that she had the Queen's ear and eventually falsified notes from the Queen to the Cardinal. The notes were signed Marie Antoinette de France; however, French queens used only their given names.

After using her invented relationship with Marie Antoinette to swindle the Cardinal out of a substantial sum of money, she convinced him that the Queen wished him to act as an intermediary, purchasing the diamond necklace from Boehmer and Bassenge. Jeanne acquired the necklace, but the Cardinal's payment was insufficient and the jewelers approached the Queen. With the scandal made public, a trial began. The Cardinal was acquitted, but several others, including Jeanne de la Motte, were sentenced. Regardless of the lack of the Queen's involvement in the diamond necklace affair, many in France believed the Queen had engineered the scandal to discredit the Cardinal and further her own self-interests.

The Revolution Begins

By 1786, the French government was nearing bankruptcy. French involvement in the American Revolution had been quite costly, but court expenditures were also high, ranging from Louis' coronation to Marie Antoinette's wardrobe. The Queen had also spent a great deal on her gardens and renovations at the Petit Trianon. In fairness to her, while the Queen spent freely, it should be noted that she was largely unaware of the state of the nation's treasury.

In August 1786, the Controller General of Finance presented the King with a plan for financial reform. Calonne had already instituted measures to reduce court spending, and his plan would increase the taxation of the rich and church, thereby not adding to the burdens on the poor. The King and Controller General called the Assembly of Notables, which offered the King the opportunity to pass his reforms without calling the Estates General.

Calonne

However, while the Assembly of Notables was expected to support the resolutions, they did not. The Controller General of Finance was dismissed in April 1787. The financial challenges drove the King into a deep depression. He began indulging excessively in both food and drink during this period. Letters to America's Minister to France, Thomas Jefferson, suggest that the King hunted half the day and was drunk the remainder of it. While this may be an exaggeration, the King certainly drank more than was reasonable by the standards of his day.

In May 1787, Etienne de Lomenie de Brienne, Archbishop of Toulouse, was appointed Controller General of Finance, with Marie Antoinette's support. Brienne continued a number of cutbacks in the court, but court spending totaled only 6-7% of total national spending. By 1788, the King agreed to call the Estates General, including members from the nobility, church, and middle classes, but did not take action to do so. Instead, the May Edicts were issued, in an attempt to allow the King to legislate changes and reforms without the consent of Parlement. Eventually, in August 1788, the crown formally called for the assembly of the Estates General. Brienne hoped to increase the representation of the Third Estate but was replaced in August 1788 with Jacques Necker, who, along with Marie Antoinette and the King, believed the Third Estate would side with the crown.

Adding to the challenges, the winter of 1788-9 was extraordinarily severe. While the nobility enjoyed sleighing on the ice and snow, the people suffered terribly. The summer of 1787 had provided poor harvests, and the hard winter led to high bread prices for the poor. In May 1789, riots broke out in Paris, as workers faced fewer jobs and higher prices. Clashes between French royal troops and the people of Paris would continue during the early summer.

The French Revolution is often described as starting with the Estates General convening in May 1789. A month later, as the King and Queen mourned the death of the Dauphin in early June, almost every member of the Third Estate, who had been locked out of the Estates General on June 20, gathered in a Versailles tennis court and took an oath to remain in session until they had a constitution in hand. Though the Third Estate was unaware, it is likely they had been locked out because the King and Queen were mourning the Dauphin, not because of nefarious plans by the royals to take action against them. Recognized by the King on June 27, by July 9, the Third Estate renamed itself the National Constituent Assembly and began drafting a constitution. Necker, a favorite of the people of Paris, was dismissed by the King on July 11, inciting significant anger.

The Tennis Court Oath

On July 14, 1789, today celebrated as Bastille Day, a large group stormed the fort-prison of the Bastille in Paris to seize arms and ammunition. The Bastille had only a few residents, but remained a potent symbol. Neither the King or Queen took much notice of this event at the event, but the Comte de Noailles brought a full report and by July 15, 1789 the situation was clear. The Queen encouraged the King to use the military to put down the revolutionaries, but he refused.

A private discussion was held and it was agreed that a number of members of the court should flee, including, among others, the Polignac family, and the Comte and Comtesse d'Artois and their children. The d'Artois children would inherit the French throne if the Dauphin died. Both the King and Queen wept at the departure of the Polignac family but carried on correspondence until their deaths. Louis and the Queen considered leaving Versailles, but opted not to, later expressing regret for this decision. On July 19, the King recalled and reinstated Necker.

Accepting the changes in the country, the King gracefully accepted a symbol of the Revolution, the tricolor cockade on July 27, 1789. During the late summer and early fall, the National Constituent Assembly undertook substantial legislative change. The Assembly eliminated serfdom, made a declaration of the Rights of Man, and eliminated censorship, creating a free press. However, political change did nothing to alleviate hunger, and bread riots continued.

Prise de la Bastille, by Jean-Pierre-Louis-Laurent Houel

The Royal Family Taken Captive

As the National Assembly kept working toward writing a new constitution, market women began a march toward Versailles on the morning of October 5, 1789. The market women, traditionally allowed some access to the Queen, had several demands. They intended to demand grain or flour in the face of shortages and high food costs, as well as forcing the King to accede to certain aspects of the constitution that would reduce royal power.

Engraving of the Women's March on Versailles

The royal family began their day quite normally. The Queen was at the Petit Trianon with friends, possibly including Axel von Fersen, while the King hunted. But word came that afternoon that the mob was on its way, and while some in the court wanted the Queen and children to leave for a more secure palace twelve miles away, she refused.

A single woman was allowed to speak to the King, pleading their cause. He agreed to order the release of two stores of grains, providing that order in writing. The King, growing concerned by the situation, also agreed to sign preliminary agreements regarding the constitution. However, by that evening, thousands were gathered outside the palace, and the mob no longer consisted just of market women. Armed brigands had joined the mob, along with a number of other men and women.

Although thousands of National Guardsmen under the orders of the Marquis de Lafayette were positioned ostensibly to defend the Royal Family, early in the morning of October 6, the gathered mob stormed the Queen's bedroom, but she escaped to the King's chamber, via a secret staircase that had been constructed to facilitate marital relations between the young couple. Their goal was a direct attack on the Queen, and though she escaped, two of her bodyguards were killed in the assault. Forced to leave the Palace, the royal family was accompanied not only by those gathered outside Versaille, but by the heads of those killed in the attack on the Palace, born aloft on spikes. The mob forced the King, Queen, and their children to move into an unused palace in Paris, the Tuileries.

While the royal family had not used the Tuileries in some time, it was inhabited by a large number of royal servants and their families. Built in the 16th century, the Palace was in considerable disrepair. Over the coming months, the family had furnishings brought from Versailles and continued daily life, much as it had been in Versailles. The Queen continued to order new dresses from her favorite dressmaker, Rose Bertin, and the family was granted a generous allowance by the National Assembly and had revenues from their own estates. The Comte and Comtesse de Provence and the King's sister, Elisabeth, were also forced to leave Versailles, and the two living aunts also took up residence in the Tuileries. The Comte and Comtesse de Provence retired to their own palace.

The family continued to gather for diplomatic affairs and regular family dinners, but the King's depression worsened and he took no actions on their behalf, even as the Queen sent messengers throughout Europe requesting aid. The Queen continued many of her own duties and hobbies, from charity work to playing billiards with the King. The family was guarded by members of the National Guard, but they were allowed a great deal of freedom during the first summer of their confinement. Still, they took no action to escape.

Over the course of the fall and winter of 1790, the situation for the royal family worsened. Political intrigues continued, with some, including the Princess Elisabeth, calling for civil war. Conflict within the Church added to the challenges. Publications on the Revolution ranged from serious texts to, not surprisingly, vulgar pamphlets. The aunts left the Tuileries in February 1791, causing a great deal of controversy. Discussions of escape increased, particularly as the state took a greater interest in the Dauphin.

In June 1791, the royal family attempted to escape, with the assistance of Count Axel von Fersen. Preparations had began in December 1790, when the berlin, or large carriage, was ordered. The berlin would include cooking facilities, a toiletry case, chamber pots and other essentials, making it a relatively luxurious means of transit. On the night of June 20, 1791, the royal family fled the Tuileries disguised as servants, while the servants disguised as nobles, and they were accompanied on the first leg of the trip by Fersen, who continued with them for approximately 16 miles before being sent back to Paris by the King. The King had also refused to take along any other experienced soldiers, perhaps condemning their escape to failure. Travelling in a large single carriage, the King was recognized approximately 160 miles from Paris at Varennes, and the National Guard returned the family to the Tuileries. The royal family was met with near silence by crowds as their carriage returned.

By early fall, the constitution was complete. The King, somewhat unwillingly, voiced his public support for the new constitution in September 1791. While the constitution included some provisions with respect to the King, it included none for the hated Queen. Louis XVI took an oath to support the constitution and share power with the Assembly, and the following April, under the orders of the Legislative Assembly, the King declared war on Austria. That only made the Austrian Queen's position more tenuous, and distaste for the royal family, particularly the Austrian Queen, continued, with a mob calling for her death in June 1792.

France's initial attempt at a constitutional monarchy was a fiasco in its first year, with the Legislative Assembly dissolving into chaos. With the government in shambles, an empty treasury, and an undisciplined army and navy, French citizens could riot without fear for their safety. On the night of August 10, 1792, a mob stormed the Tuileries and forced the royal family to flee and beg the Assembly for safety and protection. A massacre followed the King's departure, perhaps as the result of his failure to order a cease-fire as they fled, as the revolutionaries or sans-culottes killed many within the palace. In the wake of the attacks that night, the French monarchy was officially dissolved in September 1792.

Depiction of members of the Paris Commune storming the Tuileries Palace and massacring the Swiss Guards

The family spent that first night in a few rooms in a nearby sixteenth-century convent. As a response, the Assembly, listening to the wishes of the Paris Commune, had the family imprisoned in a medieval complex, known as the Tower. The Tower consisted of the Great Tower, a rather run-down palace and the Small Tower, a prison-like building. It was a far cry from Versailles; the rooms were poor and infested with vermin, and the walls in Marie-Therese's chamber were decorated with pornographic engravings. The family was still permitted to live together and was relatively well-treated, but allowed only a few attendants, including the Princesse de Lamballe. They did have access to books, needlework, and even a small dog. Even at this late date, receipts reveal the family received generous meals, as well as some clothing purchases during their imprisonment.

Chapter 4: Madame Capet

While the royal family had been allowed a few attendants when they took up residence in the Tower on August 10, by August 19, the Paris Commune began interrogating and trying royalists for a variety of crimes against the state. The royal attendants were taken to the prison of La Force, and on September 2, 1792, the family heard cannons throughout the city. The prisons were being attacked and many of the royalist prisoners, not only in Paris, but also Versailles and Rheims, were massacred. While not killed immediately in the attacks of September 2, the Princesse de Lamballe refused to swear an oath to the state on September 3, 1792 and was thrown to the waiting mob. She was killed within minutes, and though the specifics of her death are somewhat unclear, her head was placed on a pike and carried before the windows of the Tower.

In early October, the King was removed from the Queen and children and taken to the Great Tower. The family was still allowed to eat together, but access to a number of items was restricted. The Queen and children moved into rooms in the Great Tower at the end of the month, which were nicely furnished and freshly decorated, but the respite in the Great Tower was short. By the end of 1792, the trial for the King, called Louis Capet in court proceedings, had begun, and on December 11, 1792, the King was taken from the Great Tower. The children were, at the King's behest, left with Marie Antoinette, now merely Madame Capet. The family had little news of one another and on Christmas day, Louis XVI wrote his will, giving the care of the children to his wife.

Naturally, Louis' trial was a judicial farce. While the royal family was offered sanctuary in the young United States, this option was refused and an immediate death penalty imposed after the King was convicted of high treason. Of course, the King had to die, not for his crimes, but to preserve the new Republic of France, who feared that a restoration of Louis XVI to the throne was an obvious threat. The King was told of his impending death on January 20, 1793, but he was at least to be granted the mercy of the newly invented guillotine, which was meant to offer a swift and sure death, unlike the hangman's noose or executioners axe. The family was allowed to say goodbye before Louis was led to Place de la Révolution. As Louis was brought onto the scaffold, he was placed near a pedestal that had previously held a statue of his grandfather, Louis XV. Allowed to speak, Louis told his former subjects, "I die perfectly innocent of the so-called crimes of which I am accused. I pardon those who are the cause of my misfortunes." Though he wished to say more, he was cut off by a drum roll ordered by Antoine-Joseph Santerre, a general in the National Guard. Quickly thereafter, the guillotine was put to use, and some accounts of the execution suggest the guillotine did not successfully behead Louis on the first attempt. Upon his death, as his blood dripped to the ground, people in the crowd rushed forward and dipped handkerchiefs in the former king's blood.

The Execution of Louis XVI

Chapter 5: Widow Capet

Marie Antoinette, now called the Widow Capet or simply Antoinette, was devastated by the loss of her husband. In early 1793, even while she continued to hope for a possible exchange of prisoners or release, her health began to deteriorate. It is believed she may have been suffering from the early stages of both tuberculosis and uterine cancer, and she saw the doctor for convulsions and fainting fits.

Already failing, Antoinette was devastated by the removal of her son in early July 1793, and the former queen was herself arrested and transferred to the prison at the Palais du Justice during the night of August 1, 1793. While her cell in the prison was less luxurious, the more public accommodations allowed her access to priests and others. Her jailers were kind and even relatively indulgent, allowing her good quality food, mineral water, and access to books. A plot to free the Queen in early September led to somewhat harsher conditions as well as long interrogations.

While she conducted herself well under duress, the decision had already been made, and her "trial" was even more of a sham than her husband's. The revolutionary government saw the former queen's execution as essential to cement their place and unify the revolutionaries. To that end, the former Queen was accused of a host of trumped up charges, including throwing orgies in Versailles, sending millions of livres to Austria, plotting to assassinate the Duke of Orléans, having her Swiss Guards massacred in 1792, and, worst of all, sexually abusing her son. To that end, her young son was coached by authorities to turn against her and level charges of sexual abuse. While she was allowed legal counsel, she was given less than a day to prepare a defense against charges whose origins came from libelles, the 18th century equivalent of tabloids.

Antoinette remained composed during the proceedings until pressed about the sexual abuse charge leveled against her. To that point, when asked why she had remained silent regarding that charge, the doting mother countered, "If I have not replied it is because Nature itself refuses to respond to such a charge laid against a mother." After more than 30 hours of trial over two days, Antoinette was convicted and sentenced to death. She was allowed pen and paper to write a letter to her sister-in-law Elisabeth, but she was not granted a priest to make her final confession or privacy to change her clothing. In her letter to Elisabeth, she wrote of her clear conscience and her love for her children, but the letter would never reach Élisabeth.

Princess Elisabeth

On October 16, 1793, the former Queen had her hair cut off and was paraded through Paris on an open cart. The woman placed into the cart for the final journey to the guillotine was nothing like the young girl who had come to Versailles. By now, the Widow Capet was thin, pale, and suffering from serious blood loss as the result of her gynecological difficulties. Nevertheless, she remained quiet and dignified on the cart ride and as she mounted the scaffold, her courage intact. Her last words were reputed to have been "Pardon me sir, I meant not to do it", due to the fact she had inadvertently stepped on her executioner's toe while mounting the scaffold. Marie Antoinette was executed shortly after noon, and her remains were dumped in an unmarked grave.

Depiction of Marie Antoinett's Execution

The fate of many of those close to the Queen or involved with the royal family was equally tragic. Louis XV's mistress, Madame du Barry, was executed by the new regime, and the Duchesse de Polignac died in exile not long after Marie Antoinette herself. The former princess, Madame Elisabeth, met her fate at the guillotine in May 1794, and Louis-Charles died, possibly of tuberculosis, in 1795. Only the young Marie-Therese lived, freed through negotiations in 1795. She married the Duc d'Angouleme, her first cousin, but her marriage and life were not happy. She had no children, leaving Marie Antoinette with no descendants.

Chapter 6: Marie Antoinette's Legacy

History does not remember Marie Antoinette kindly. Executed during the French Revolution, the queen is remembered as a woman who danced and threw grand parties while the people starved. While there is no evidence she ever spoke the words, she is often credited with having said, in response to the hunger of the people, "Qu'ils mangent de la brioche," or "Let them eat cake". Indeed, the quote comes from Jean-Jacques Rousseau's *Confessions,* in which he writes,

"Enfin je me rappelai le pis-aller d'une grande princesse à qui l'on disait que les paysans n'avaient pas de pain, et qui répondit : Qu'ils mangent de la brioche." **(English)** *Finally I recalled the stopgap solution of a great princess who was told that the peasants had no bread, and who responded: "Let them eat brioche."*

Rousseau never named the great princess who he attributes the quote to, and historians don't believe it was an actual quote. Nevertheless, the words have since been affixed to Antoinette, and though the words were not hers, there is truth in the sentiment. The Queen of France was so greatly removed from her people that she could not conceive of the poverty, hunger and deprivation that tore apart eighteenth-century France. Taxes were high and the French people were angry. Marie Antoinette was not to blame for the challenges of France, but she became a scapegoat for many of the struggles that led to the French Revolution, often called *Madame Deficite,* named so because of her spending habits. Some of her contemporaries, including Thomas Jefferson himself, blamed Marie Antoinette of single-handedly sparking the French Revolution and the subsequent Reign of Terror.

In the centuries after her death, tabloid style speculation about her life continued to be standard fare, and instead of attempting to portray Antoinette in an accurate light, stuff written in the 18th and 19th centuries continued to focus on her spendthrift ways and her supposed sexual liaisons with Fersen and possibly others. It was only in the 20th century that more evenhanded biographies of Antoinette appeard, and generally the search for historical accuracy is far less sensational than the gossipy rumors that preceded it. No matter how sympathetic biographers have been, they haven't made a dent in the standing Marie Antoinette continues to hold in pop culture across the West.

There is still argument over the depiction of Marie Antoinette, who some viewed as a good and loving mother who was tragically tone deaf and became a victim of the Revolution's growing radicalism. Of course, others viewed her as epitomizing the excesses of royalty, and clearly this latter viewpoint has taken hold more strongly. In most depictions and media references, from historical novels to movies, Marie Antoinette is portrayed as the ignorantly out of touch Queen. Though other French royals, like the "Sun King", spent just as unconscionably, it is the powerless Marie Antoinette who has come to symbolize the problems associated with France's absolute monarchy. That legacy doesn't seem likely to change anytime soon.

Bibliography

"Marie Antoinette and the French Revolution." Public Broadcasting Systems. http://www.pbs.org/marieantoinette/index.html (accessed on June 16, 2012).

Campan, Madame. "Memoirs of the Private Life of Marie Antoinette." Modern History Sourcebook. http://www.fordham.edu/halsall/mod/1818marieantoinette.asp (accessed on June 16, 2012).

Covington, Richard. "Marie Antoinette." Smithsonian Magazine. http://www.smithsonianmag.com/history-archaeology/biography/marieantoinette.html?c=y&page=1 (accessed on June 16, 2012).

Fraser, Antonia. Marie Antoinette: The Journey. New York, NY: Anchor Books, 2002.

Weber, Caroline. Queen of Fashion: What Marie Antoinette Wore to the Revolution. New York, NY: Picador, 2007.

Printed in Great Britain
by Amazon

34817885R00030

FOR UX

SWE_ _
SPOT

Communicating User Experience
to Stakeholders, Decision Makers
and Other Humans

MIKE NEWMAN

Published by Authority Connect in 2021

Authority Connect is an imprint of OMNE Publishing

A catalogue record for this book is available from the National Library of Australia

Any opinions expressed in this book are exclusively those of the author and are not necessarily the views held or endorsed by the publisher or others quoted throughout. All the information, exercises and concepts contained within this publication are intended for general information only. The author does not take any responsibility for any choices that any individual or organisation may make with this information in the business, personal, financial, familial, or other areas of life based on the choice to use this information. If any individual or organisation does wish to implement the steps discussed herein it is recommended that they obtain their own independent advice specific for their circumstances.

Print and Kindle production by OMNE Publishing

Cover and typeset by Evan Shapiro

This book is available in print and ebook formats.

CONTENTS

FOREWORD

What makes a great user experience?

No matter the industry or business they are in, more people today expect, and often demand, a great experience when interacting with a (usually digital) product or service, and more of your colleagues are asking, "How will this affect the user experience?"

Whether it's seeking information on the web, completing a transaction through an app, or engaging with a contact support person via live chat, user expectations are ever-higher and this directly affects the trust and loyalty we have towards any product or service we are interacting with.

As more and more businesses embrace innovation, moving increasingly towards smarter technology solutions like Voice Interfaces, Artificial Intelligence and Machine Learning, it's no surprise then that User Experience (UX) is a term that is commonly thrown around in strategy meetings, where decision makers discuss the importance of hiring the best talent to execute their vision. Their goal is to attract and retain more customers to give them an edge over their competitors. Competitors who are, of course, doing the same thing.

Needless to say, UX designers are always in high demand and can command an enviably high salary too. A quick search in Google alone suggests there are now close to a million UX designers around the world, and you don't have to look too far to find businesses offering courses to learn or upskill in UX.

Some of the courses available to those wanting a UX career or those seeking to extend their knowledge in user experience aren't able to cover all the scenarios you will encounter, though. Successful UX designers are not only required to have great hands-on skills but also need the acumen to expertly take those around them on the journey of how to do it properly and explain why it is necessary. Attaining the skill to convert colleagues into UX advocates is not an easy thing.

There are a lot of UX professionals who have gained vital experience on this during their careers, but an individual honing their skills has to be lucky to work with these experts to learn and grow.

I had the pleasure of working with Mike and have seen him put such exceptional skills into action. From properly coaching a new stakeholder and their project team into the UX process, to his comprehensive application of his UX design skills. Add to that, his insistence on a collaborative process and his welcoming approach to mentoring made it all the more ideal that he should compile this guide.

There is a lot of reading material out there in the world of User Experience. A lot of them are essential reading. While they cover a lot of the necessary hands-on skills of ideation and designing, most don't cover the some of those critical soft skills.

This book will become a must-have for anyone growing their UXpertise in dealing with difficult stakeholders and challenging situations. These are just some examples of the situations Mike has covered: convincing that stakeholder who knows more than you that you are not just there to wireframe; facilitating that challenging workshop with multiple people with competing business needs; and importantly, how to evangelise UX in your organisation and get support for UX from the top down.

So, what makes a great user experience?

A great user experience *designer* does. And that's why you will want this book as a constant companion to your career. It's one UX book that won't gather dust.

Kevin Raccani
Digital UX CX Manager

Kevin Raccani started his career in graphics in 1981 producing a range of projects in the sphere of digital development, including app, web, mobile, marketing, gaming, broadcast and other developing technologies. He was working in the experience of users before UX was a common term. Today, he is known as one of Sydney's leading UX professionals, having led and managed UX teams for some of Australia's largest organisations in the telecommunications and education sectors.

PREFACE

This book is written to help mentor other User Experience (UX) professionals in applying their craft within their businesses. It is also helpful for those who are in business and want to understand more about how UX fits within their organisation and how to start improving the user experience of their product or service.

Do you ever find yourself having to justify why user experience matters inside your organisation?

In working with other UX professionals, I identified a common industry pain point — communicating UX to stakeholders, managers, teams and colleagues in a way they understand or care about. As a UX professional, it can often feel like you are swimming against the tide as you constantly strive to justify your craft. Organisations consist of people with different career objectives and backgrounds, and many of them may not know much about UX, might be misinformed about what it is, or may not care that much about it. This book will help those UX designers who are facing those challenges, or those in a UX team who want to transition to a more leadership position, to learn how to start speaking the same language as their stakeholders and clients. They will become more successful and gain more leverage for their practice.

I interviewed a number of successful UX professionals to understand the secret behind how they communicate the value of UX inside their organisations and to their clients, to understand how they gain and maintain buy-in for what they do. They cited many frustrations and challenges in applying their craft, including:

- An unwillingness by a business (or client) to invest time and money in discovery or proper user validation testing
- Business requirements dictating the solution rather than being driven from the customer's need

- A business that is misinformed about UX. For example, not under-standing that UX is not the same as UI (User Interface), or believing the primary purpose of UX is to just deliver wireframe specifications
- And many more....

What you'll get from this book

This book is for forward-thinking UX professionals looking for ways to improve their craft. The end game for me is to empower you, the UX designer, to become a highly- successful professional; to transition you from a hands-on designer to a strategic leader. This will entail having the skills around communication and trust in at least equal proportions to your practical skills around UX design.

I have put together some key strategies to mentor you to become more successful at UX communication within your organisation. Some of the things you'll get from this book are:

- Insights from other UX professionals and some context on why certain problems exist, and some useful ways to approach them
- Communication techniques and strategies to help get straight to the point with your UX design message
- Some simple formulas designed to help colleagues or business teams become more aligned around your UX practice, and help you become better at applying your craft within your organisation

I have been discussing this topic with many other UX designers over the years and this book combines my own learnings with those of other profes-sionals I met along the way or have worked with (thank you everyone, you know who you are). If you are a UX designer at the start of your career and looking for simple advice in dealing with stakeholders, or an established UX professional seeking a way to improve your soft skills to advance your career further, then this is the book for you.

INTRODUCTION

'Adaptation' as a UX designer is key — it's not just designing a product for the end-user that's important for success, but also being able to shape your process to fit within your working environment.

MY STORY

One of the many challenges we all face as UX designers is that the business we work for often doesn't understand UX, or how to apply it into their existing ways of working. I'm a UX professional with a design background of 20+ years. Over the years, I have been lucky enough to work with some amazing professionals and lead some truly awesome UX design initiatives across a range of industries including telco, media, B2B, travel, construction, government and retail. I started out in product design in the early 2000s (or web design as the vast majority of us called it back then *cringe*) and in those days, it was very different to how it is today. This book is not meant to be a history lesson, so I won't go into details, but there is a common thread that remains today — the user. Human Centred Design (HCD) was a big thing even back then, and usability testing was a solid user-centric practice.

When web design was still in its infancy, the smartest businesses quickly realised that the key to getting customers to adopt a new website or software product was designing an interface successfully, which meant understanding its usability from a real user's perspective. Barclays Bank in England was one of the early pioneers of such user-centred design practices, and it is where I began my user-centric design career.

As Head of Design and Production in their Interactive Design Centre in London, I oversaw many interactive design and production activities within the design team, including the evolution of their new brand identity on the web. My boss at the time introduced me to a methodology called Rapid Application Development (RAD) which was used to iterate product applications for their customers. The approach incorporated a lot of user research, low fidelity prototyping, usability testing and managing the work through to a fully polished and implemented product.

Since then, I have honed my UX skills over many years and consider myself to be an end-to-end UX designer by trade and an experienced UX design consultant by choice. My primary goal now is to help businesses improve their digital products by making them more meaningful to their users, and to help other UX designers master the art of communicating UX to clients, stakeholders and other decision makers.

THE ART OF COMMUNICATING UX

One of the key skills I am constantly refining (and is a focus of this book) is the art of communicating UX design within organisations to stakeholders and decision makers, as it is integral to achieving success as a UX designer. An important aspect of this type of communication is being able to adapt to fit the individual quirks of an organisation and its culture. Every business is different as it is essentially determined by a group of unique human beings who have been thrown together to help an organisation achieve a specific goal. No matter how big or small the organisation, its eco-system is always made up of people interacting with each other — many professionals with varying experience and cultural backgrounds, with individual personal and career agendas, and different personalities at play. This means 'adaptation' as a UX designer is key: It's not just designing a product for the end-user that's important for success, but also being able to shape your process to fit within the organisation's environment.

If you are starting out in UX, navigating this business-human landscape can be hard to grasp. Over the years I have worked in many different types of organisations, both client-side and in agencies, and have worked with, for, and managed other UX professionals along the way. Along my journey I noticed a common pain point for many fellow UXers — communicating UX to stakeholders, managers, teams and colleagues can at times be a real challenge, sometimes even harder than the challenge of designing a product itself. For example, if you have been taught 'lean start-up' methodologies but find yourself working in a corporation that doesn't operate like a start-up, it may feel like an insurmountable challenge to do your best work.

WHAT IS UX?

As a UX designer, how many times have you had to answer that question during a job interview? Even for an experienced UX professional, it can be a challenging one to answer particularly as the person asking already has some preconceived ideas about what it is, and they may not be the same as yours. These days, everyone seems to have an opinion on what a good user experience is. And that can be frustrating when your stakeholder challenges your design with a broad-brush comment like, "I don't think that's a good user experience" — a comment that is based purely on their own subjective viewpoint.

In the beginning, describing UX was simple, but the landscape of design has changed so much, and the user experience is so ingrained in business and other disciplines, that it has become much more complex to describe. UX is now a multi-disciplinary practice that consists of a lot of different skills. It is described in the same sentence as visual design or interface design, interaction design, information architecture and usability. It crosses over into development and delivery, research and data, psychology, accessibility and content and marketing. And of course, it is also interlinked with other related practices and processes like customer experience, service design, design thinking and agile development. It's no wonder then that a UX designer can often feel their work is misunderstood or that their organisation is misinformed.

These days, the reality is that UX design is rarely the responsibility of the UX designer alone. Because so much contributes to the overall experience of the end product, UX actually becomes the responsibility of whole teams of people who are working together on the project. Whether it's an app or a website or something else, there'll likely be designers, developers, project managers, senior managers and clients, all of whom are contributing to and influencing the end product. Each different perspective also brings a different dialect. Think of the language of a designer versus the language of a developer versus the language of a business stakeholder; they may be using the same words, but each have their own subtle differences which can lead to confusion, frustration and misinterpretation. This is why communication is a critically important part of UX.

If you find yourself struggling in this area, recognising that you're not solely responsible for every design solution is an important step. You need to change your mindset from 'I am the only designer in the room' to the 'I am the facilitator of many designers in the room'. As a design facilitator, you are responsible for leading the design process, and managing the space in which design occurs; you are not solely responsible for the design outcome itself.

PICKING YOUR BATTLES

I try to attend the UX Australia conference most years, and at a recent one I saw an interesting presentation by a UX consultant from Perth.[1] One of his presentation slides was entitled "Pick your battles" with a diagram of a see-saw on it. On one side he had the words "uselessly agreeable" and on the other side of the see-saw he had the words "being a jerk no one can work with".

This slide resonated with me because, as a UX designer, it's very easy to find yourself pressured towards that "uselessly agreeable" end of the see-saw, where the business is telling you to design something — an idea or a feature that someone has already invested time and budget in developing — but the implementation of this feature is being dictated by a business solution rather than based on proper, valid user research. To let that order go through unchallenged is essentially to be told by the business what the user wants, negating the true purpose of having a UX resource in the first place.

But if you fight your way to the other side of the see-saw, challenging it, or insisting that more user research is required, you could easily end up arguing until you're blue in the face. You may feel like you're getting nowhere, like you're banging your head against a wall trying to get your point across, and then the business ends up doing it anyway because timelines and budgets are already agreed upon. Welcome to one of the real-world challenges of UX design.

---

[1] Delalande, P. (2019, 27-30 August). *Break the rules* [Conference presentation]. 2019 UX Australia Conference, Sydney, NSW, Australia. http://www.uxaustralia.com.au/conferences/ux-australia-2019/presentation/break-the-rules/

WHY DO I CARE ABOUT THIS SO MUCH?

I care about it because earlier in my career, I felt like I was on that see-saw going up and down. There were days when I felt absolutely beaten and couldn't get my message through in the right way and let decisions go that I didn't believe were good enough. Or found myself arguing constantly with people around me and getting nowhere; it was like I was talking a completely different language.

And the other reason I care so much about this is because I've worked with so many good UX designers over the years and many, in fact I'd say *all*, at some point, struggled with that one point of communication: Selling the value of their work, and getting their ideas across in an effective way.

FINDING THE SWEET SPOT

I realise now that I learned those crucial lessons the hard way. I spent years trying to debate, convince and defend design decisions and getting nowhere, or being too agreeable and letting stuff go. These days I realise I can't make someone change their perspective just by arguing a point, and bad design always comes back to bite you at some stage, so over time I have adapted my communication style to fit better with the people around me.

I have written this book because no qualification will teach you the soft (or hard) skills around how to align your business communication with your users in an authentic and powerful way. By using some of the techniques in this book, you should get more interest in the practice of UX, and ultimately build more trust and backing from your stakeholders to do more UX work in the future.

BECOMING AN EVANGELIST

As well as knowing how to design, UX designers also need to know how to evangelise their work within the organisation where they work. This means not only listening to users and understanding their needs and pain points, but also knowing how to articulate those users' mindsets in a way that stakeholders can relate to. The goal is to be *the voice of the user* at every opportunity to create empathy for your users' needs, behaviours and expectations within the minds of your stakeholders; and any other people you work with who have a say in the experience you are designing.

It's important therefore to recognise that UX is not just about the user — it's also about the business. Every UX designer either works within a business or for a business and recognising that balance is the key to creating successful outcomes for customers. If I were to draw a Venn diagram of two intersecting circles — one circle with the words "business goals" or "business requirements" and the other circle with the words "user needs" or "user preferences" — where those two circles intersect in the middle is the sweet spot. That's where a true sweet spot UX designer works: As a conduit between the user and the business.

UNDERSTANDING THE ART OF SWEET SPOT UX DESIGN

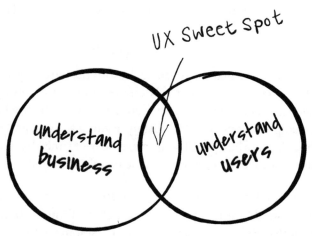

Mike Newman © 2021

A good designer is able to get in the heads of their users by understanding their needs and goals and knows how to design great experiences for them. But a *great* designer can do that whilst also understanding what is important to their stakeholders and helping the business achieve *their* goals as well.

There have been a lot of UX books written and many of them focus on processes and methodologies. This book takes it further because it is about applying those processes and methodologies within an organisation to the best effect. It's about helping you, the UX designer, to become better at selling the value of user experience within your business (without being a salesperson) to help you find that sweet spot between the user and the business in which you work.

In addition to the communication side of things, there is another important aspect of being successful, and that is mindset. I believe self-confidence and maintaining a positive attitude is always extremely important for continued success. No matter where you are in your UX career — whether you're just starting out or are very experienced — you can still find yourself sensitive to feedback and need to find ways to manage your confidence whenever you step outside of your comfort zone. Being in the right frame of mind, whether it's standing up and presenting, receiving feedback on your work, or working with challenging stakeholders, the right mindset is absolutely essential for success.

QUICK TIPS

Throughout this book you'll find useful tips in these panels. These will highlight key points, activities, and some different perspectives to consider.

CHAPTER ONE

GAINING CONFIDENCE AS A BUSINESS PROFESSIONAL

A few years ago, I discovered the concept of the "Hero's Journey" when I watched a YouTube video about Joseph Campbell's monomyth of popular culture.[2] It presented the idea that popular culture often follows a similar hero narrative of adventure and personal transformation, and I realised that this narrative is also applicable in our careers. Every person in their professional career should be able to relate to the idea that in life we face many obstacles and crises that create struggles we need to overcome. In overcoming a struggle, we transform and become a better version of ourselves. This is part of our personal growth — our hero's journey if you like — and we should embrace these struggles rather than retreat to our status quo.

"Real self-confidence is not reflected in a title, an expensive suit, a fancy car, or a series of acquisitions. It is reflected in your mindset: your readiness to grow."

- Carol Dweck [3]

Writing this book was a real turning point for me professionally. Publishing, presenting and talking about it was a real challenge to overcome and was a huge milestone in my professional career. It was such a challenge because I've not been as comfortable talking about myself as talking about other people. I've had a lengthy career in UX design which spans over 20 years and, in that time, have focused mainly on promoting the businesses of others, more than the business of myself. In fact, I've made a pretty good career out of talking about other people (users), whilst not talking about me.

---

[2] https://www.youtube.com/watch?v=GNPcefZKmZ0
[3] Dweck, C. (2017) *Mindset: Changing the way you think to fulfil your potential* (updated edition). [Kindle]. Robinson.

My UX career really began in the banking sector in the UK, where I started with usability testing for online retail banking applications. Since then, I've presented product solutions, findings and recommendations, conducted workshops with businesses and team members and, on agency-side, I've sold concepts and ideas to businesses and clients talking about product design from a user's perspective. As far as this goes, I've been really good it. But I always knew that I struggled when the lens was turned on me. Talking about myself and my achievements has always been difficult, and there's a reason for this. I stumbled upon the reason whilst attending some life coaching lessons to help guide me through the process of writing a book.

What I uncovered during those sessions goes way back — right back to a pivotal moment in my childhood. I must have been about 11 or 12 years old, and I was in the first year of secondary school in England (the equivalent of year seven in Australia). I had always been interested in the creative arts, science and technology; they were the three things that I enjoyed the most and therefore did well at. That's why I gravitated towards UX because it is a kind of creative science — it encompasses a bit of both. Design, innovation, problem solving, solutioning and data analysis is all a mishmash of right- and left-brain activity.

In my first year of secondary school, I achieved some great creative outputs and received some excellent marks, including a creative story that was published in the local paper with a prize attached. Shortly after, I produced a painting that my teacher thought was amazing, and I won an award for it. Every year the school gave out this particular award for art. By school terms, it was a fairly prestigious award as it had been created by the head of art to acknowledge and encourage young talent, and it was only awarded to one student per year. That particular year, it was me, and I believe I was one of the youngest ever to win it. I remember being incredibly proud of my achievement and that I was recognised for my artistic talent.

I was asked to accept the award during morning assembly. It was a big day for me as I had to stand up on stage for the first time. I was nervous, but also proud of myself, and felt as though it would be a defining moment for my future. It was quite a big school, so there were a lot of students in assembly that day. As I stepped onto the stage, I remember the smiling faces and applause from the teachers at the front. The headmaster shook my hand

and the head of art handed me the award. It was a really proud, defining moment — well, at least for a second.

As I looked out across the crowd of other kids looking back at me (it felt like millions at the time) my stomach folded over and over, collapsing inwards. Rather than applause and cheers, all I heard was laughter and jeering. Then one kid shouted out, "Loser!" and my heart sank like a lead balloon. I felt sick inside and I just wanted to be swallowed up, never to experience that thing called recognition again.

So, what I uncovered during my life coaching sessions was, that particular moment had a big impact on me — it was probably the instant I started to avoid praise and began to gravitate away from attention and recognition by deflecting it elsewhere. I became uncomfortable talking about myself and my achievements for fear of the same level of ridicule.

In my earlier professional days, I believe I had been trying to express all my achievements through the success of others as this felt much more comfortable. When I contributed to improving something — a better product for example — I had been mostly happy to let others take the credit for my contribution. Even when kind people went out of their way to recognise me for my work, I had always been too modest to accept it. Instead of saying, "Thank you" I would prefer responses like, "I only did xyz" or, "It was more of a team effort".

Whilst that last statement is true (things usually *are* a result of a great team effort), that phrase for me was a diversion — a cop-out to avoid the limelight because it had been hardwired into my psyche — as I didn't want to stand up in front of people and talk about myself in case I got jeered at again. And I resisted writing a book for many years, for exactly the same reason.

Whilst I struggled with my sense of legitimacy earlier in my career, I now challenge it head-on, and always try to give myself credit for the success I've had throughout a long and fruitful design career where I have always pushed myself forward. I've worked with some amazing clients and co-workers across many sectors, I've helped produce a number of great digital products for customers across different industries, and more recently I presented at the pre-launch of this book at Jane Turner's Authors Showcase at the State Library of NSW in Sydney. In addition to that, I've enjoyed advising others by encouraging younger, less experienced UX designers entering into the UX community to do what they need to do on their own journey of success — one of the reasons why I wrote this book.

With all that in mind, writing, marketing and promoting this book has become my hero's journey. This book includes many aspects of dealing with the real-world struggles that a UX designer might face in an organisation, or when working for a client. And whilst I am still learning as well, I hope this book will help you focus on how to stand up and back yourself and your achievements, whilst maintaining the respect and recognition of others in your team. That's why the focus of this book is on communicating within the UX industry and how to get your point across in the right way. There is an important section on interacting with different types of people, whether they are demanding stakeholders, difficult team members, or just co-workers with different communication styles.

There are a lot of books available about the processes and the methods of doing UX work and research. These processes and methods, and the specific tools that UX designers use, are not included in any detail here. They are all important and I'm not suggesting changing any of those things; this book is really a supplement to help you to improve your communication in a way that is useful to you, your business, and your users. This book is for those UX designers who need guidance on how to take their business on the journey of understanding the value of UX, using the art of communication, effective collaboration, and mindset.

WHY IS THIS IMPORTANT?

Learning the right communication techniques is critical to being able to broker the right results for the clients or the organisation you're working for which, without mastery, can hold you back in your career. There are plenty of UX professionals who lean towards being deeper-thinking problem solvers than extroverted communicators (myself included), and deep thinkers usually need time to gain confidence in presenting and collaborating in order to build their own sense of legitimacy as persuasive UX facilitators. So, this book is helpful not only for those UX designers who struggle to thrive in a heated debate or argumentative landscape, but also for those who want to build more confidence, credibility and authenticity within their organisation, or across the organisations that their own business provides services to, so they can elevate their career and success.

OWN YOUR HERO'S JOURNEY

Everyone's hero's journey in UX is different, as every UX designer faces their own unique challenges and hurdles to overcome. In this chapter I will share my friend's journey — a challenging road to becoming a credible and very well-respected senior UX designer which was a journey more challenging than mine.

She moved to Australia from Hong Kong about 10 years ago and built a successful career here in UX but, on her hero's journey, she faced many challenges. She started working in Hong Kong for a 3D-design company before moving to Australia to study design. After graduating from university, she got her first proper design job with a software start-up. It felt very different to working in Hong Kong — the most obvious difference being adapting to working with Australian colleagues.

The first challenge was that the lifestyle and social situations were unlike Hong Kong. She immediately noticed the subtle differences in Australian workplaces, such as how normal it was to participate in a lot of casual 'chit chat' and that took some getting used to, culturally. In the kitchen people would ask, "How are you?" and, "How was your weekend?" or, "What are you planning for the weekend?" For her, the first part of adapting to being a designer in Australia was not the work itself; it was learning the subtleties of communication and cultural differences that we all take for granted in the place where we grew up.

People were nice to her, and they probably didn't register how difficult it was for her to adapt. She remembered being uncomfortable about the 'chit chats' because her English wasn't as good as the people with whom she was conversing. It required a lot of effort to speak as she often did not know what to say. She didn't understand the language within the language either; "What is a good chit chat that people are expecting?" she recalled. The analogy she used when describing it was that she felt like a kid learning manners for the very first time.

Her first jobs were very visual design-oriented and a lot more geared towards implementation and less towards the user research side of things. Her goal was to transition into the UX space but to do so, she had to overcome a number of key communication challenges. It was not as easy as receiving a brief, working in isolation, then presenting her work, as was the case with her previous design roles. Making the jump from visual design to UX design required a lot more collaboration with different types of colleagues, teams and departments — something that was a massive hurdle for her. Ultimately, it required a lot of intense communication; not just talking and discussing designs, but also properly interpreting business requirements and translating them into something meaningful that was in line with user expectations, and then communicating back to stakeholders to gain buy-in.

MEETINGS AND PRESENTATIONS

One of the first things she said to me about the challenges of being a designer was, "100% of your work gets presented and get judged and critiqued by managers" which made presentations a very daunting task from the beginning. The language barrier was obviously a contributing factor to this. For her first few years as a UX designer, she attended many meetings and workshops where she wasn't sure what the expectation was. She felt much 'smaller' in the meetings than everyone else and was self-conscious as her English wasn't perfect. Her non-English speaking background meant she was often unclear about what she was responsible for in the meeting and was therefore often afraid to speak up.

And the most important part — and this is a key empathy point for all — in fast-paced meetings she would still be thinking when it was time for discussion. She was disadvantaged because she needed to translate and process the information in her head in Chinese before she was able to translate her thoughts and responses back into English for a discussion. This is a huge challenge when you're trying to master the art of UX, which is essentially a communication-focused role.

Because the structure of her sentences had to be carefully constructed in her head, she adopted a very matter-of-fact response to people, and this made her feel even more uncomfortable. Having to think about her manner and tone, and the context of what she was saying, all led to a massive shift in confidence from speaking in her native language to speaking in a foreign language in the country where she was now working. There is a cognitive mindset process at play within all of us, but her language barrier made her feel as though people didn't trust her experience, which started a vicious cycle. Whilst her ability was sound, she often felt like a more junior member of the team, which then affected her confidence even more.

Anyone who has experienced moments where their self-esteem has been damaged in some way during their career should be able to identify with the immense problems she had to overcome in order to become the highly successful UX professional she is today. For this alone, I am in awe of what she has achieved.

EMPATHY

In a fast-paced business meeting, if you are from a non-English speaking background, this puts you behind the eight-ball straight away. It's an important point to remember for anyone in business; in addition to language barriers, there are also cultural differences that should be part of everyone's empathy radar.

CULTURAL BIAS

There was a speech at a UX Australia conference I went to where the presenter, Farai Madzima,[4] talked about cultural bias in design, and discussed the variety of communication styles in different business cultures around the world. It was a fascinating topic, and a real insight for me at the time when I was working in a UX role in Australia, dealing with international stakeholders across Europe, USA, Japan, China, Malaysia and Singapore. Knowing that there were inherent differences in how meetings were expected to be conducted made a huge difference to my ability to communicate effectively within my own language limitations.

Business culture and language aside, I believe you should always give time for someone to formulate a response — pause and encourage an opinion

---

[4] Madzima, F. (2018, 28-31 August). *Can being African make you bad at design? Cultural bias in design* [Conference presentation]. 2018 UX Australia Conference, Melbourne, VIC, Australia. http://www.uxaustralia.com.au/conferences/uxaustralia-2018/presentation/Can-being-African-make-you-bad-at-design-cultural-bias/

even from those who may appear to have nothing to say. This should also be part of your empathy radar by acknowledging the diversity of personality types. For example, an introverted thinker whose natural inclination is to internalise information before speaking, is very different to an extroverted thinker who naturally externalises in order to process information. Both are important, and both should be acknowledged and respected.

GAINING MORE CONFIDENCE

Now going back to my friend's hero's journey. How did she make the jump from visual designer to a successful and well-respected senior UX designer?

When I met her, she was part of the UX team I was leading. She made friends and did her job well, but still gravitated towards the more 'hands-on' desk work as it was comfortable for her and didn't require exhausting levels of communication and collaboration. I recognised her unique design ability and made sure she was able to contribute to discussions, taking the time to really listen to her thoughts and ideas, provide suggestions, and challenge her. Essentially, I became her mentor.

She told me that it was a pivotal time in her career, and that I should take some credit for it, so I will. I introduced her to a lot more UX and got her involved in a number of workshops. At that point in her career, her horizon was beginning to broaden, and she was starting to take more interest in the research and strategic side of design. After working with me, she was able to throw herself in the deep end and at some point, after I left my role there, she started a new job at a large financial corporation where she worked in a team of about 20 UX designers. From there she was able to observe how they worked and what was involved in the full-time job of a UX designer in a large corporation. She saw that they had a lot of meetings with stake-holders and conducted extensive customer interviews, and whilst it was a concept she now understood, she still felt she hadn't fully grasped it yet.

UX COURSES FOR CONFIDENCE

Shortly after this, she did a UX crash course which are now very popular. The course included theories and information about UX methodologies and how to come up with an idea and execute it. The focus was on the principles of 'Research, Design, Test'. But for her, it wasn't enough training to make the jump. It didn't reflect the reality of working in a job with other designers in a corporate business landscape, where there are real business problems and stakeholder engagement. In the real world, you never work on your 'own idea' and you face stakeholders who can be extremely resistant, she said.

TOOLS OF THE TRADE

The other aspect that can't be ignored is mastering the tools of the trade.

Software skills usually aren't covered in UX courses, nor are they covered in this book, but it's an important point to raise here. Learning the tools of the trade in UX and UI gives you the skills you need and the confidence to know that you can always deliver. So, whether it's Axure, Sketch, Figma, XD, or whatever else, mastering your tool of choice is an important aspect of maintaining your ability to deliver, and therefore maintaining your confidence.

In the real world you have to deal with real people. You might have to take a concept and present it, at which point there might be a debate or a discussion, and then you might have to come up with a design solution that's potentially desirable and test it. But then someone might say any of the following:

- We can't do it because it's not feasible or viable
- I don't think it's a good user experience
- I know my users wouldn't use that
- You didn't test with enough users
- We don't have enough budget to test with users
- There's not enough time for research
- Just come back to me with some wireframes or mock-ups based on your professional opinion

Or even just plain old, "No".

"There's no crash course to teach you how to overcome those real-world challenges", she said. She realised, after doing the UX course, that she had already gained a lot of base skills and what she was lacking was the confidence and communication skills to apply what she knew in the business world.

The course was a good way to qualify herself in her own mind and gave her permission to believe she was capable of being a proper UX designer — to overcome her imposter syndrome. But the main learning was the realisation that the biggest barrier was actually her confidence and mindset.

Eventually, she moved to New York and worked for a very busy and demanding agency. She was required to make a presentation every day as part of her job. Pushing herself out of her comfort zone into a tough and competitive environment was a defining moment in her career — she simply had to get good at it very quickly. And she did. Ultimately this was where she gained her biggest confidence boost as a UX designer.

I believe self-confidence and maintaining a positive mindset is a challenge to everyone, regardless of how they may appear from the outside. No matter where anyone is in their career, successful or not, everyone is sensitive to feedback, and everyone needs to find ways manage their own self-confidence when stepping out of their comfort zone. We are all human and we are all constantly striving for self-worth in what we do. That is why communication and mindset are key topics of this book.

I asked my friend if, knowing what she knows now, she was to go back in time and give her younger self career advice in UX, what would it be?

Her answer was:

- *Make the effort to make friends* — It takes a long time to open up to people, especially when you struggle with the language. Try to adapt to the lifestyle as quickly as possible.
- *Learn the culture* — Really embed yourself in the culture of the organisation. If you are from a different cultural background, then try to experience the culture in the language you are working, not just study it academically.
- *Master the tools of the trade* — Having good software skills gives you the confidence to know that whatever happens, you can always deliver.
- *Throw yourself in the deep end* — This will force you to learn and adapt quickly.
- *Find a mentor* — Find someone who is approachable and willing to teach you what they know. You can learn more from having a mentor

than any course, and it can help you become more comfortable talking about UX.

HAVING A MENTOR

Having a mentor can be very beneficial. You can go about it in an up-front way and ask a senior manager, "Would you be my mentor?" Some people would be responsive to that, but a mentor can also just be a friend at work or even an ex-colleague in whom you can confide. The simple approach is to identify someone you trust and say, "Can I get some advice from you?" Many people, myself included, are happy to share their knowledge.

BEING A MENTOR

You shouldn't wait for someone to ask you to be their mentor. No matter what stage of your career you are at, there are always others who will benefit from your advice. My friend from Hong Kong I spoke about in the previous chapter was someone I mentored; not because she asked for it, but because I recognised her desire to learn and knew she would benefit from some guidance. I believe a key trait of being a leader in any profession is to look to help those who are trying to learn what you do — give them the confidence they need to succeed themselves.

GROUP MENTORING

Mentoring doesn't have to be face-to-face, and it doesn't have to be for a single person. I am a part of a several groups either formed by myself or by other people I have worked with over the years. They are people I trust and can flick a question or thought to and get an answer back. I can easily message someone and say, "Do you have a few minutes for a call?" or, "Does anyone know the best UX tool to use for xyz?" I might sound as though I'm stating the obvious, but these relationships really are critical in transitioning yourself from a designer to a lead role. You can never do anything on your own, whether it's getting a new job, learning a new process or getting someone to read chapters of your new book. (Thanks guys!)

CHAPTER TWO

TRANSITIONING FROM A UX DESIGNER TO A STRATEGIC UX LEADER

The journey I am taking you on represents the transition from being a process-driven UX designer to becoming a strategic UX design leader. Being a UX leader means applying both hard skills (the tools and methods) and soft skills (communication, empathy and understanding) in equal amounts. The hard skills are very important, and you learn these as you progress through your career. Mastering UX tools and methods gives you confidence as a UX designer but transitioning to a strategic UX leader is really about mastering the soft skills around communicating a UX vision, evangelising it, listening to feedback and managing conflict. This requires hard work, dedication and a willingness to adapt.

"Your primary role should be to share what you know, not to tell people how things should be done."

– Steve Krug[5]

To use a metaphor from *The Wizard of Oz*, to take you and your business or client along the yellow brick road to UX success, you need to adopt three main journey goals: be like the scarecrow who wants a brain (learn to get into the headspace of your users); be like the tin man who desires a heart (develop empathy towards your co-workers and clients); and be like the cowardly lion who seeks courage (build the courage to step out of your comfort zone).

In the following pages, I will help you to develop some essential UX soft skills — a business-focused communication style that will start to resonate with stakeholders. You will find pointers to help align business thinking with UX thinking — to align your organisation to the way they should be commu-

---

[5] Krug, S. (2014) *Don't make me think, revisited: A common sense approach to web usability.* [Kindle]. New Riders.

nicating with their customers. Using the learnings and approaches laid out in this book you will start to build trust and establish a solid foundation to move forward from. For me, the end game is to empower you to be a highly successful UX professional, and that entails having the skills around communication and building trust in at least equal proportions to the hard skills you already have around UX design.

NOT BASHING YOUR HEAD AGAINST A WALL

My background as a UX professional is littered with design debates that I often lost in the early days. I spent a lot of time banging my head against a brick wall, telling clients and business stakeholders how they were wrong; that they were not the user and they needed get out of their own head and into the heads of their customers. I'd wear myself out trying to communicate in words alone the value that providing a great user experience would bring but was often faced with blank indifference.

Thus, I learnt that being a good communicator is not about having the gift of the gab; while that is useful, the critical characteristic of a good communicator in UX is being a good listener. Having empathy will get you even further. You already know that you can't understand your customers' needs or preferences if you do not listen carefully to what they tell you or observe what they do. The same applies to your organisation — how can you understand their needs if you are too preoccupied with arguing about your design decisions to listen to them properly?

I believe the hardest part of being a UX design professional these days isn't keeping up to date with the ever-changing methods and systems that are available. The hardest part is creating an environment where the businesses you work for are able to understand the true value that a deep and thorough approach to UX represents for the end user. Without establishing this level of understanding with your business or client, you will likely struggle to get stakeholders or clients on board in the first place, or you will struggle throughout the process of working with them. This will be to the detriment of the results you could have brokered for them, and to your career as a UX leader.

Something I have tried to focus on in my career is helping other, less-experienced, UX designers establish good UX practices amongst the people that they work with. The client or business unit they have been assigned to may lack knowledge of what UX really is, and its true value. Just knowing the processes and practical skills alone aren't enough; I've seen plenty of good UX designers who have the skills to provide a lot of value with their craft, and become frustrated when they realise that, to others in the organisation, it's not so important.

Many UX designers are problem solvers, not politicians, so getting into a situation where they have to debate their self-worth is not ideal. I hear from many UX designers that they often get into confrontations about their work and they feel an expectation to "Defend a design decision". But often this term is just another name for a debate. Saying, "You must" or, "You should" is usually met with a counter argument.

EVANGELISING UX

OK, so we all know that there is a whole heap of reasons why UX is important, but when counter arguments kick in, you often feel like you're fighting a losing battle trying to make people understand the importance of what you're doing, and why it's crucial for their customers. It might not even be a senior manager; it might be someone in your team, a peer, a developer, a visual designer, a project manager or even another UX designer. There is a whole range of people that you work with in your UX career who you could encounter resistance from.

When you get to the point where you're always trying to tell people how they should be doing UX, instead of them just asking you to do it, then you are familiar with the challenges I have outlined. Whilst frustrating, I find it useful to remember that it is normal human behaviour — people are usually so absorbed in their own world and what is important to them. Allowing them to see the value of UX is really about shifting their mindset to be more empathetic — opening the door to empathy and helping them through it.

Later in this book I will help you establish a UX perspective that you can apply to your business and to other team members who may be less mature in their UX thinking. For some organisations, this means going back to basics. Stakeholders, senior managers and many clients want to get a high-level understanding of what you're proposing without going into granular details, so the purpose is simply to help them understand what you're trying to do, and covering off some simple misconceptions that they might have around UX.

In explaining what you do and why it's important, I've always found it best to focus on educating, without being patronising, and framing what you do in terms of a practice. Rather than focus on deliverables such as a wireframe or an interface design specification, frame UX as a toolkit of methods that you use to help improve the user experience and communicate that back to the business or client.

TAKING THEM ON THE JOURNEY

I often say that UX is a creative science. On the creative side, there is a lot of visual work: concepts, ideation, sketching, innovation; and on the science side there is: psychology, test methods, data and analysis. So as a practice, it's a bit of a spectrum from the creative end to the science end. And if you're hired as a UX designer within an organisation, you will mostly likely encounter people who don't know much about that, or they might have a predetermined idea about where UX sits on that spectrum. You might work inside an organisation that sees it more as a visual thing — more interface design — or it could be seen as more about information architecture or delivering specifications to a developer. In fact, UX is likely to encompass all those things, particularly if those things are important to making the end user experience better.

So, across that spectrum there is a whole range of different things a UX designer will be responsible for, and that includes educating and evangelising the role of UX within the business where they work. Success in this endeavour is not just talking about what UX is, it's also about experiencing it. Collaboration is a great way to do this by getting relevant parties involved in the process. There are many resources available about this, including Jeff Gothelf's book, "Lean UX" where he discusses transitioning from a hero-based designer into a design facilitator.[6]

In my earlier career, I experienced that transition from design hero to design facilitator. I realised that trying to be the design hero, who is expected to have all the answers, is too challenging when dealing with difficult characters

---

[6] Gothelf, J. and Seiden, J. (2016). *Lean UX: Designing great products with agile teams* (second edition). [Kindle]. O'Reilly Media.

in an organisation. Perhaps there are some really big egos in the room, or people who have strong opinions who don't like to be told otherwise, and in those scenarios, you may not be influential enough to successfully challenge them. I recognised that design facilitation was probably more helpful, and less prone to failure.

But being a design facilitator and running design workshops is not easy either. You still have to negotiate your way through the different personalities in the organisation. It can be challenging if a key contributor is just not interested in what you have to say about UX. Perhaps your manager expects you to be the expert already and wants you to just tell them what the user experience should be. Or perhaps they are personally attached to a business requirement or feature they like and don't want it to be challenged, or they simply resist your attempts to draw them into a workshop because they consider it a waste of their time.

SWEET SPOT UX WORKSHOPS

My next book focuses on some simple but effective and lean design workshops that can be introduced slowly without being overwhelming or intimidating to you or your participants. Following the steps in the book, you will be able to foster better alignment in your team, whilst building trust and credibility in what you do, and also personal confidence in facilitation. Whether it's stakeholders, a single team member, or a whole team, wherever you encounter a problem and need more UX alignment to move forward, this will help. So, watch this space.

CHAPTER THREE

Taking the business on the journey of UX requires many things, but it *is* easy to start. On the following pages are some recommended steps to focus on when starting out in a new organisation or on a new project. Depending on the maturity of the business, some will require more work than others. And depending on your own confidence level, you can use these either as a reference or as a check list to help you progress in your UX career.

"Find a group of people who challenge and inspire you, spend a lot of time with them, and it will change your life."

– Jeff Golthelf [7]

UNDERSTANDING WHO YOU ARE TALKING TO

As highlighted earlier, one of the many challenges we all face as UX designers is that the business we work for often doesn't understand UX, or how to apply it into their existing ways of working. UX is a very bespoke profession, full of acronyms and expert methodologies so it's not surprising that it is misinterpreted by those we work with. When dealing with our users, we frame our words and questions so they are appropriate to their persona, but in a business environment we often don't.

Becoming a sweet spot UX designer is really about being sensitive to your organisation's way of speaking, as well as your users — acknowledging that your organisation's language is different to yours, and to be successful you need to empathise with your co-workers as well as your users.

---

[7] Gothelf, J. and Seiden, J. (2016). *Lean UX: Designing great products with agile teams* (second edition). [Kindle]. O'Reilly Media.

UNDERSTANDING YOUR STAKEHOLDERS

Getting to know your users means also getting to know your stakeholders. It can often help to set aside time for 'stakeholder safaris'. These are essentially groups of stakeholder interviews which will help you get to know your decision makers and understand where they are coming from. Establishing a connection with your stakeholders helps build trust and credibility; it is an opportunity to explain what you do and how you can work together. You will be able to use the material from these interviews to help bring extra value and understanding to your *team personas* mentioned later in this chapter.

Where to start

A stakeholder interview is one of the most effective ways to kick off a new project, to help them discover what they really want and for you to get inside their heads. There are a number of free templates available online to get you started.

If you don't feel comfortable asking for a formal interview, you could just organise a catch up over a coffee, a one-on-one meeting, a phone call, or a corridor chat whilst discussing a piece of project work — anything to open up the channels of communication between you and your stakeholder. Your key aim is to learn more about the business needs and cross-pollinate your world with theirs.

UNDERSTANDING YOUR CO-WORKERS

A colleague of mine asked me to include some tips on *how to speak the same language as their development team*, as well as their stakeholders. I puzzled over this request for a while as to me, each team I've worked with is different, consisting of different people from different backgrounds and disciplines, so speaking to developers about UX seemed to be something you learn instinctively. But during my research, I came across several articles and discussions about this topic, including a video by Garrett Goldfield[8] which had some great advice.

Goldfield says you should take the time to understand your co-workers' priorities and goals so that you can explain UX to them in ways that are

---

[8] https://www.nngroup.com/videos/communicating-ux-colleagues-organization

clear and easy to understand, much like you do with your users. With users, we are mindful of the language we use, but with co-workers we often don't extend that same level of empathy to them.

He says that for developers, rather than just handing them something to implement, a good approach is to invite them into your world by getting them involved in the design process itself so they can understand the rigor, methodology and data used to drive the design decisions. This helps cross-pollinate your world with theirs and leads to a shared level of understanding of each other's goals. I do this a lot, and it also helps them to directly see the benefits of their development work when real users provide positive feedback like, "This application is really useful and will save me time."

This all falls into the category of "co-designing" and I mention it a lot in this book as it's an essential approach for aligning your UX with your co-workers. But remember that understanding their needs and pain points is also extremely important so that you can learn to use the words and vocabulary that resonates best with them.

CREATE TEAM PERSONAS

Having empathy for your co-workers is very important. Understanding your co-workers' needs and pain points means you can become more sensitive to them and know how to communicate better.

A great way to understand who you are talking to within your organisation is to create some team personas. These are similar to the ones you might create for your users, but they are focused on the needs and motivations of your co-workers and stakeholders. If you can understand the goals and priorities of the product owner or project manager in your team for example, you are better equipped to work together. They may be sensitive to timelines and their mindset fixed on how to deliver product increments quickly and move on to the next feature. Knowing this helps you be more attuned to what they are trying to achieve.

You can use any format you're comfortable with or you can follow the worksheets included in this book as a starting point.

For example, Goldfield points out that with developers, they may be sensitive to having to recode a piece of work. Their mindset might be to deliver code quickly and accurately and therefore it may be frustrating for them to revisit (or iterate) their work over and over. So, when communicating with developers, he advises framing UX activities in terms of "driving more accurate designs", which results in "less rework in the long-run".

He extends this advice to cover other roles: when communicating with timeline-sensitive project managers, he says we should speak to them about how UX provides an opportunity to validate designs to catch unforeseen problems early; and when communicating with revenue-driven executives, he says to seek opportunities to describe UX in terms of Return on Investment (ROI) and customer loyalty.

This got me thinking, and after further discussions with my colleagues about *how to speak the same language as their development team*, we came up with a template for some simple team personas, to help UX designers understand their co-workers' mindsets.

Using Goldfield's co-worker examples, the developer, the project manager, and the executive, your team personas might look something like this:

TEAM PERSONA WORKSHEET:
THE DEVELOPER

What is their role?

E.g. Front-end development in an Agile Development Team

What are their goals?

E.g. Delivering working code quickly and accurately within the sprint

What are their key frustrations or pain points?

E.g. Having to refactor code due to unforeseen changes in the design

How best to communicate?

E.g. Developers may be sensitive to potential recoding so we should communicate that the UX activities drive more accurate designs, which result in less rework. Include them in design workshops, acknowledge their ideas to establish an investment in the outcome, and involve them in more user feedback sessions.

TEAM PERSONA WORKSHEET:
THE PROJECT MANAGER

What is their role?

E.g. Project managing the team in respect to planning, design, and execution of each digital project

What are their goals?

E.g. Motivating project team members to complete and hand-over deliverables on time and on budget

What are their key frustrations or pain points?

E.g. Unclear or undefined requirements, unexpected changes in scope

How best to communicate?

E.g. Project managers will likely be sensitive to timelines. We should speak to them about including proper UX initiatives across the overall project timeline and explain how it provides an opportunity to validate designs to catch unforeseen problems with the product that would otherwise cause the team to miss important milestones.

TEAM PERSONA WORKSHEET:
THE EXECUTIVE

What is their role?

E.g. Direct, plan, and coordinate operational activities for the business, focusing on their business area of expertise

What are their goals?

E.g. Directing and motivating their business area in what needs to be done at a high-level

What are their key frustrations or pain points?

E.g. Not enough profit or cash

How best to communicate?

E.g. Executives are likely to be concerned about revenue. Seek opportunities to describe UX in terms of ROIs and customer loyalty.

Of course, these are just examples. You need to do these yourself, and there are many more....

CO-DESIGNING WITH YOUR CO-WORKERS

Be sure to become familiar with your team personas so that engaging in activities with them becomes more seamless and aligned. To successfully get your co-workers on board with your UX work is not just about understanding what their motivations are, it's also about taking them on a journey into your world of UX. It's no accident that I have mentioned a few times the benefits of running co-design workshops. These are a great way to get your team involved. The design process should ideally be as much about working together, and allowing individual voices to be shared and heard, as about coming up with a design solution.

I cover this in more detail in the next chapter, and in my next book you will find some key workshops I have developed specifically for alignment between your team persona groups and your UX practice.

CHAPTER FOUR

Whilst UX is now a mature field and is well known in most business circles, it is an unfortunate fact that whilst we may make the effort to get to know our businesses needs and motivations, too often they still don't fully understand what we do. So, navigating other people's ignorance or disinterest in UX is the primary obstacle for UX designers to overcome if they want to transition from being 'do-ers' who deliver wireframes and specifications, into 'strategic thinkers' in leadership roles.

"The way to go from discord to harmony is to go from concentrating on differences to concentrating on similarities."

Anthony Robbins [9]

I spoke to a number of UX professionals to better understand some of the key pain points they face in dealing with UX in the business world. In this chapter, I have collated and categorised their responses into the top three most common UX pain points, and some of the common solutions used to address them. In the next chapter I will look at some specific communication techniques that you can use to help bring them on-side and *take them on the journey.*

---

[9] Robbins, A. (2003). *Unlimited power: The new science of personal achievement.* [Kindle]. Free Press.

UX PAIN POINT #1

Obstructive bias
(Driven by ignorance, an unwillingness to listen, and a lack of understanding)

UX designers I spoke to said they find it frustrating when stakeholders say they already know what the customer wants and show little interest in any facts to the contrary. Or sometimes it's the opposite, where they seem overly interested in the facts but really, they are using it as ammunition to debunk the data with comments like, "Why did you only test with six users?" or, "That's not reliable research" or, "You're just telling me what I already knew." This can be exhausting to repeatedly justify your findings.

The other aspect to this can be that in many organisations, stakeholders simply don't fully understand UX, or even the digital space in general. That's okay, of course. Who are we to assume everyone has the same perspective as we do? What this means, however, is that a UX designer may struggle, battle even, to explain the purpose of UX, and only get blank looks and comments like, "Oh I don't get that UX stuff, that's your job" or worse, "Can you just design a page that looks like this?"

Misconceptions about what UX is

In conversations with other UX designers, they said that clients or stakeholders often believe UX to be something it is not. For example, they may think it's the same as visual design or UI design. Of course, the visual component always plays an important part of the experience of a product but *interface design* itself is mostly the deliverable that happens towards the end of a UX process. This "deliverable" mentality puts downward pressure on the research-end of UX which is critical to its success. As one UX designer told me, it was either their project manager who seemed to push for completed designs or wireframes early on so they could tick it off in their project plan, or their delivery-focused product owner who wanted to close off stories as quickly as possible in the sprint.

The important aspect here then is highlighting and educating co-workers and stakeholders on common misconceptions and finding ways to slot it into the existing delivery process. It's important to educate co-workers on how UI plays an important role in the experience of a product, but it is not in and of itself the whole user's experience.

Ignorance leading to business bias

UX designers I spoke to said that a lack of understanding of the value of UX often leads clients or stakeholders to not respect valid UX research and in particular can be resistant to proper testing with real users. The "deliverable" mentality often means they want to jump straight into a solution based on what they think, without fully understanding the context of the problem they are trying to solve for the customer.

Many felt this was in fact their main frustration — trying to overcome the inherent business bias within their organisation. Senior managers often become attached to their own ideas and are then unwilling to listen to the needs of their users when it negates their viewpoint. A belief system is thus born of the notion that they are already the expert of their business, and therefore an expert of their customers too. As a UX designer, simply saying, "But you are not the user" will never unravel the ego of a determined stakeholder who believes they know how the user experience should be.

UX PAIN POINT #2

Multi-directional project priorities that don't support UX

Other UX designers I spoke to said that some stakeholders have a tendency to prioritise ideas they *think* will work (or just like them more) over solutions that are based on solving real user problems, with evidence to back it up. It seems common for a business requirement to dictate the solution rather than articulate the customer's needs and pain points.

A lack of desire to invest in proper UX may come down to the impact UX initiatives have on other project priorities. Therefore, it can be seen as a roadblock — something to slow progress rather than something that saves the business time, effort and expense later on. The mindset that a UX designer needs to instil in stakeholders or clients is that a business requirement is actually merely an assumption that needs validating with real users. But this is not always an easy spiel.

Being overpowered by business decisions

Because of this, the UX designers I spoke to felt that stakeholders can be obstructive to their work — playing politics and laying speed bumps in the design process which in turn does not allow them to fully achieve their UX goals. Organisations can place an emphasis on the 'Highest Paid Person's Opinion (HiPPO)', rather than the customers.

Because stakeholders and senior managers feel they are paid to make decisions, feature priorities can often be based on seniority, position and accumulated knowledge of the industry. This can lead to decision-making that is not always customer-centric and in turn becomes a huge frustration for many UX designers. Overcoming this is an art that requires communication skills: You cannot simply argue with a HiPPO. Instead, you have to learn how to influence decisions rather than try to make them yourself and argue until you're blue in the face.

UX PAIN POINT #3

Time constraints means no budget for UX

Digging deeper, some UX designers I spoke to said that the underlying issues are budget and time constraints. A common perspective is, "Why should I spend $x on discovery, when I already know what I want?" and, "It's an MVP (Minimum Viable Product), so let's just get the development team to build it and we can always change it later", which is not the purpose of an MVP at all, of course.

In their minds, stakeholders or clients may have unrealistic expectations about how much time is needed for UX, especially time-consuming activities like 'UX discovery' that may require interviews to be conducted and results to be synthesised. So, it's often the first thing to go in relation to cutting down costs and time, and the MVP discussion, whilst valid, can often be used as a scapegoat.

When the emphasis is on squeezing a project timeline to meet cost, it's easy to think of user testing as unnecessary, and pressing deadlines often squash the value of UX in the overall development process. That is why lots of the UX designers I spoke to had to face the very real challenge of, "Sorry, we have no budget for user testing." This is the most frustrating statement for a UX designer to hear, because we all know that once you remove the "user" part of user experience design, you literally are left only with "design" and that's like driving a car with no wheels.

The secret to overcoming this problem isn't a simple one. Of course, using leaner testing methods (like corridor or guerrilla testing) can sometimes get you over the line, but there is still the need to re-educate the business on the role that UX should be playing. UX is not a 'deliverable'; it's a practice that sits adjacent to all work and helps feed information from the customer across the entire project to ensure the most successful outcome to the customer, and therefore delivering enormous value to the business. Again, this requires expert communication skills.

ADDRESSING THESE PAIN POINTS THROUGH COMMUNICATION

I asked a number of senior-level UX designers how they typically address these pain points and below are some of the approaches they take. I will expand on a number of these to provide you with some useful techniques to navigate some common UX pain points when communicating the value of user experience inside the organisation where you work.

Speak to them about it in plain English

UX designers I spoke to said that being able to explain what UX is, is paramount to success. UX designers need to be able to explain it in layman's terms to everybody in a way that is non-patronising, especially to those who have a good knowledge of business and design. They say that if you ask five different people what UX means, you'll get five different answers. So, I asked five different UX designers how they explained what UX is in layman's terms, and their answers are below:[10]

- Designing the whole experience for the user of a product (e.g. a website or an app) to make it as easy to use and as enjoyable as possible.
- The art of building simple and user-friendly products by empathising with the people who use it.

---

[10] Anonymous answers taken from a user survey. Newman, M. (2020, 28 January – 5 February). *7 Questions for UX Designers*. [User Survey].

- Researching how users behave and what they need, then designing experiences for them on the web, in an app or anywhere else they interact.
- Helping businesses to transform ideas into products, making sure the product improves people's lives/solves a problem/brings value, while increasing business revenue.
- Designing apps and websites — the way they look and how you click and tap around it.

None of these explanations are wrong. In fact, I like all of them, but what I have discovered is that no one complete sentence will lead to an "Ah-ha" moment that a non-UX person will remember when you walk away.

Highlighting common misconceptions

UX designers say the word 'design' can often mislead clients and stakeholders into thinking of UX as the 'look and feel' — a design artefact, a screen to be implemented by a developer that can easily be delivered towards the end of the project. It's easy to assume that the function and ease of use are *features* of the design that are built in automatically as part of the look and feel and are determined by the UX designer's own expertise. This has contributed to the common mindset of, "When I hire a UX designer they will work with my developers to build what I want in a way that customers will like".

In order to overcome this misconception, UX designers often dedicate time to explain and reiterate the value of the user experience and the proper process — sometimes in person, sometimes in meetings, and sometimes in dedicated UX presentations. This is a process in itself; an educational process that takes time and patience.

Highlight the risks and talk about ROI (Return on Investment)

When speaking to stakeholders such as senior managers, UX designers often say they have to adopt a style of language that stakeholders can relate to. The things that typically concern senior managers for example, might be risk management, cost or waste reduction, and the bottom line — the ROI dollar value of the product, which includes investment in user experience initiatives.

In this case, justification for proper UX work takes time. When educating stakeholders on the monetary value of user experience, many UX designers say it helps to show how it has benefitted in other projects they have worked on. This could be outcomes achieved on recent projects within the same business, or something from a previous role. Failing that, they will draw from the vast amount of research available — case studies and articles with statistical evidence and graphs — that show how conducting UX research early and often actually saves money.

On top of that is the conversation of risk — reframing their interactions so they are speaking the language of budget and ROI. They can be completely up-front about that or find ways to highlight the risk in general conversation; but they try to put the onus on their stakeholder to carry the risk.

Here are some examples of conversation techniques that UX designers use:

Without effective customer feedback, we can't build it properly.

"We can proceed without user testing, but unless we are sure on x, y and z, we may end up having to completely re-do it all later and that will cost extra time and money in development."

The concept is incomplete, would you like to do more testing or take the risk?

"This is my best guess based on what we know today, but x, y and z are still unanswered questions, and we know are key to its success. Would you like us to investigate it further or proceed without?"

How much money are you willing to risk on your investment?

"Your budget is $x. Surely you can afford to spend $y on user testing? It's such a small amount of the overall cost and will ensure you deliver the results you intend."

These are all very good communication techniques to try. But the approach of 'UX risk' alone doesn't work for everybody and, for myself, I have found it requires a lot of trial and error in its delivery before people genuinely recognise the benefits and trust my perspective.

Create a FOMO (Fear of Missing Out) effect

Another tip from UX designers I spoke to is to use the power of what others are doing in their space to inspire stakeholders to take notice of potential success and build credibility. This can be as simple as highlighting how high-profile businesses have used UX techniques to deliver value and are now proven to be streets ahead of their competition, like Google, Uber, or Spotify. Or it can be a thorough competitive analysis. This is a valuable piece of UX work that can help identify gaps in their process and highlight the importance of not being leap-frogged by competitors. In fact, someone I met at a CX (Customer Experience) conference told me that their key stakeholders were more motivated by what their competitors were doing than any statistics he presented in a PowerPoint slide.

Guide them to their own "Ah-ha" moment

Many UX designers rely on presenting evidence as this helps gain trust and credibility in their work by highlighting the science behind it. This approach can seem like a catch-22 though — in order to show the results of your UX research, you first have to conduct UX research, and if your organisation is already resistant to spending money on UX, your options are limited. In this situation, many UX designers find themselves having to build a case from scratch. This may consist of conducting corridor interviews or guerrilla testing to gain some valuable insights that will help them highlight the problem or risk that the organisation is taking by not testing their product early, to show the value in a ROI.

This might entail enlisting the help of a supportive manager who is prepared to hand over their credit card for a small investment in coffee vouchers as user incentives or funding it themselves for the first time as a proof of concept, or by digging into available user data sources such as user feedback from their site or app, or by gathering insights from a Subject Matter Expert (SME) like a service centre operative.

TAKE THEM ON THE JOURNEY

Let them experience it for themselves

Most of the UX designers I have spoken to agree that a powerful way to educate their organisation in the value of UX is to involve them in the process at every step. In truth, there isn't a single sentence or phrase that will lead to an "Ah-ha" moment that a non-UX person will easily remember. No explanation fully addresses the common misconceptions of UX, and it won't immediately solve budget concerns, or diffuse the ego of an obstructive stakeholder who already has a solution in mind. So, the most effective way to explain what UX is, is to *show* what it is, rather than *explain* what it is.

This can be anything from interviewing stakeholders as your SMEs to align thinking between you and them, to showing co-workers videos of customers struggling with your product. Or even better, getting decision makers or project influencers to sit in on a customer interview or participate in the design process through a co-design workshop.

The commonality is that communicating UX is not a simple exercise — it takes a lot more than conversation. It requires you to take them on the journey by involving them in consulting (influencing, reinforcing), sharing articles, running workshops and UX whiteboard or sketching sessions, and pointing to outside content that amplifies the overall value.

Show them the evidence

Many UX designers agree that well-founded evidence is invaluable in winning the battle of UX. It could be as simple as showing an example of some user data in Google Analytics, or more visual data — maybe a heatmap that highlights an issue on a page, for example. Often, once they show a co-worker or stakeholder the data, they are more receptive and want to see more. But that's not always the case. If they're participating in a project that is underway and items are already in progress and plotted on the roadmap, coming in and saying, "Hang on a minute guys, there's an issue that we need to go back and test," is not always a popular thing to say.

This is where the communication and language really come into play, as UX designers need to shift the verbal emphasis from, 'testing' to something like 'quick validation' or 'sense check' when talking to their managers to show they're doing their due diligence.

Prove the value of your work

UX designers say that metrics are important to prove to their business that the work they are doing is adding value to their bottom line. People in their organisation may not realise that, when done properly, UX is completely measurable. When they start to see an improvement in the numbers, they can start to see it as a tangible benefit and that makes a huge difference in building their credibility and laying the foundation for further backing.

There are some great methods and frameworks online that are well documented: SEQ, SUS, SUPR-Q, Google Heart framework, and more; find something that works for your project. Then, be sure to get input from data enthusiasts such as a conversion optimisation specialist, a data scientist, a savvy analytics person, or anyone who has extensive expertise in data analytics to help add extra credibility and value.

I often start with a simple ground-up framework focusing on a couple of basic task success metrics. Once you have some basics in place you can start to work with stakeholders to create a dashboard that speaks to them. Your UX dashboard is essentially a communication tool reinforcing your success metrics, customer feedback, and any other supporting research that is of value to your organisation. Your goal is to establish UX rigor and highlight the success of the work you are doing in a way that is genuinely useful for your team and your stakeholders.

It's easy to start — it can be created as a spreadsheet, in a slide deck or in a more sophisticated format such as Google Data Studio. If you can find someone to support or sponsor your initiative, or an existing team that already does something similar, suggest adding in some user experience data.

SIMPLE GROUND-UP METRICS

Task success

A good metric here is SEQ (Single Ease Question) which can be used as part of a usability testing session. Alternatively, you can ask the analytics guru in the team to help you implement something that hooks into Google Analytics for a more quantitative result.

Measuring the overall experience

Establish a baseline score for what the 'perception of user experience' of your product is, or perhaps a specific key journey. Use that as a benchmark to understand how the experience is improving over time. This way, if you are measuring specific journeys within your product, you can see the impact recent design changes have had since you last tested. With this approach, it's important to get a balance between 'usability' session scores and 'survey' scores so you can weigh up the qualitative with the quantitative.

For benchmarking metrics, you can look at SUS or SUPR-Q. I like SUPR-Q because it covers usability, look and feel, trust/credibility and loyalty, which means you can talk to those points with stakeholders in a way they understand. If you buy the SUPR-Q[11] database, you can also benchmark your site or product against other businesses, but you might need to sell its value to your organisation first if they're not familiar with this approach.

Don't sweat the small stuff

UX designers I spoke to said they often have to "pick their battles" to find a reasonable balance based on the work being done. If you're Google, then it's fine to sweat the small stuff and fight for every little detail. But often, in the real world of busy corporations with competing agendas, if you try to test every little thing, you'll end up meeting increasing resistance as you will appear to be creating speed bumps for your development team. If you're launching a new widget, then test it. If you're just changing some

---

[11] http://www.measuringu.com/product/suprq/

copy on a page, you may be better off waiting until it's live and carefully listen to feedback.

A good option is to do a corridor test to gather some quick data; this is a sanity check for yourself to see if it requires more rigorous investigation. If it does, then invest the time and energy to push a bit more by showing (not telling) your concerns to the relevant persons and let them have the responsibility of taking the risk.

But also, do sweat the small stuff

The final point here is to always ensure some time is put into the post-release validation. After it goes live, diligent UX designers always check the user data and feedback or do some sort of testing to make sure it works as expected. This sounds obvious, but I find it is often overlooked. In addition to data analytics, there are some popular visual analytics tools that are often used to assist with post-launch validation including HotJar, Mouseflow, CrazyEgg, VWO, Optimizely and so on.

Depending on the size of your organisation, these tools may already be used so all you need to do is ask for access for your project. If not, then you'll likely need to write a rationale for your manager or stakeholder explaining how it will add value and save time and cost in the long run.

GETTING APPROVAL ON UX SOFTWARE

If you work for a business that doesn't fully realise the value of UX it can be hard just to validate paying for important software. This is when you need to speak the language of the decision maker by providing a compelling rationale. Here's an example of a rationale you could use for purchasing a piece of user testing software:

What is this software for?

As UX designers we use this software to do quick and easy 'lean user testing' of our prototypes with customers — it allows for remote user testing, recording user sessions, making notes and analysing findings to help improve the user experience of our digital products.

Why test with users?

- User testing helps validate (or invalidate) critical assumptions at low cost
- Testing early avoids potential re-work by adjusting designs ahead of development
- Products that focus on user testing are proven to increase customer satisfaction
- This software is used by our competitors and many other top organisations like Google

What's the alternative?

The alternative is to outsource the user testing to an agency who will conduct the sessions face-to-face in their lab. By using this software instead, we will be saving the business money by conducting the sessions ourselves, and by doing mainly remote user testing, we will also save the project team valuable time and effort.

What's the risk of not using this software?

The main risk is the potential costly re-work if we discover usability issues after development because we weren't able to test them properly with customers at the beginning. This can impact customer satisfaction, which is directly linked to our sales and revenue.

OTHER WAYS TO TAKE THEM ON THE JOURNEY

Here are a few other techniques I suggest you should try to implement – to help take your organisation on the journey of UX and build trust and credibility with your stakeholders and co-workers.

Become your customer

Acting as the voice of the customer in meetings and workshops is also key. Once you get inside the heads of your users and know your persona groups inside out, you can act as a representative of your customer, speaking as if they were attending your meeting. Without bias, ask yourself what they would say if they were there and had a voice.

Showcase your users

Your customers won't be able to attend all your meetings, so a quick user video can be a handy way to summarise something from their perspective to educate your team about a pain point or problem to solve. It's easy to fall into a business-only focus or personal preferences, so be sure to constantly remind your team members of who they are designing for. That's when you can go back to your stakeholders and say, "This is not really resonating, lets change it like xyz." For example, during a team discussion you may remind your peers, "We know that user X is time poor and doesn't want to spend 10 minutes crawling through the homepage reading detailed information when they just want to buy a widget." The point is to start the conversation from the customer's perspective, and then test your assumption.

BRING CUSTOMERS INTO YOUR WORLD

In addition to contextual interviews or user testing, inviting your customers into your organisation can be an extremely effective way of building empathy and understanding for you and your team.

TIP: Organise for some of your customers to participate in a co-design workshop for a new feature or identify representatives of your key personas to talk to your team about their needs and pain points in relation to your product.

Tailor your communication to fit the audience

In the previous chapter I spoke about the importance of having empathy for the people you work with, in the same way you would with your users. There is no right or wrong way to communicate (we are all different) but a good UX designer knows they need to put aside any bias and acknowledge that all people have different ways of communicating. For example, presenting to a room full of designers and developers is likely to be markedly different to presenting to a room of senior executives.

For this reason, when preparing a presentation, you should always make sure your audience is well considered. A time-poor senior executive may only attend for the first few minutes of a presentation so you may need to capture their interest with a high-level executive summary. If you have a Doubting Thomas in the team, they may want to drill into the details and digest all the evidence you have to back up your recommendations. Often you need to cater to both, and more.

Garner support from your wider team

As a UX designer, you need to accept that sometimes you can't take on the burden of customer needs and pain points all on your own. I believe the support you have around you of other UX designers is important. But if you work as a stand-alone UX designer (I have done this a lot), or for an agency that contracts you out to clients, then you need to ensure you build a team of supporters around you.

Many successful UX designers I spoke to recognise this and try to build alliances of support for their work, and of course for the customer whom they represent. Basically, you need as many evangelists on your side as you can get — team members you can bring with you to meetings to share their specific expertise or support.

Sometimes it's easier to garner support one-by-one, gaining buy-in within your own team first and then venturing outwards. If you can get everyone in your own team on board — perhaps it's the developer, the business analyst, product owner or project manager — once they see first-hand the benefits that UX delivers for them in their role, their support will back your goals outside of your team.

Remember, UX is not just about being the designer

To do all this is certainly a challenge. It means that UX designers need to drop any design egos you have and be prepared to truly listen to your team and ensure you always design openly, collaboratively and transparently with those around you. Building rapport with as many SMEs as you can is also important. It's good to take the time to really learn about your business by being curious and seeking out valuable connections and relationships in other areas of your organisation and encourage them to get involved in your work.

A good way to involve your co-workers is to use them as a sounding board for your UX work. Doing a peer review or a dry-run is beneficial as it helps you pick up errors before presenting to stakeholders. This is your chance to test the presentation to make sure you haven't missed anything and that the timing is right — so a 30-minute presentation to a stakeholder doesn't go for an hour.

It's also an opportunity to pick up any errors that might come back to bite you in a presentation. If a developer tells you that the database won't work in the way you had anticipated, then it's better to know in advance to save yourself (and your team) from embarrassment in a presentation.

Use what you know

Getting others across what you're working on also creates good communication and ensures a cross-pollination of ideas. Designers are good at communicating in pictures, so tap into your visualisation skills as often as you can to articulate your messages to stakeholders and co-workers. For example:

- Kick off a brief on a whiteboard (rather than emailing a document)
- Get up and draw on the whiteboard in a meeting to articulate an idea
- Sketch out a journey map or a timeline to clarify an intent

Of course, the same approach should also be applied when working remotely:

- Open up a Wiki page and collaboratively write a brief on screen together
- Schedule a quick Hangout or Jam Board session to co-design an idea
- Quickly outline an intent using boxes and lines in Google Draw or Visio

PRACTICE CO-DESIGN THROUGH DESIGN COLLABORATION WORKSHOPS

This gives co-workers and stakeholders every chance to offer input and question the work, so they too become advocates for UX within the organisation. Collaborative design is really handy because you can follow-up later and say, "Look at what *we* designed in our workshop." This is very different to presenting *your* designs and asking for *their* critique, which is polarising and encourages debate. Maintaining the rigor and discipline to collaborate throughout the whole project is important — you want to make sure you avoid surprises and keep everyone invested in the outcome at every step.

START SMALL AND BUILD UP

Mastering the art of design facilitation requires tons of collaboration and improvisation which takes time to master. Start by running workshops in small groups to learn and refine the process. Do a proposal workshop, or a small design session on a whiteboard or Hangout with another designer for 15 minutes. Then add a non-designer and build from there until you can confidently invite a key stakeholder.

One challenge when running a workshop might be dealing with difficult characters — anything from people turning up late or not at all, to a loudmouth senior manager always playing the Devil's Advocate, or the Doubting Thomas who picks apart every fine detail of your findings. But you shouldn't let these stop you as the benefits far outweigh the challenges.

Understand your audience

Collaboration techniques are about working together and allowing individual voices to be shared and heard, rather than a reliance on either an ego-driven designer or a loudmouth manager. You should always think about your communication strategy for including everyone in the room. Before presenting anything, it always helps to fully understand your audience. Have clear goals and be sure to dry-run your design presentation with peers for a sense-check on the suitability for the audience.

For a detailed-focused audience your UX storyline might look like this:
- The problem you're trying to solve and some insights around it
- What strategy or method you've adopted
- The design solution so far with initial results from user testing
- Recommended next steps including why it's important (such as suggestions for further user testing to validate xyz)

For a time-poor or executive audience, your UX storyline might look more like this:

- Here's where we were at before
- Here's what's changed
- This is what's next (further work required)

These days, there are plenty of other things to consider when communicating with your teams. For example, I find myself working remotely and dealing with international teams more frequently. The days of grabbing a few people for a physical whiteboard session seem to be diminishing. These days UX designers either have to make do with a camera pointed at their whiteboard or invest in collaboration technology. If you're not one of the lucky ones who has access to a state-of-the-art Google Jamboard, then a Wacom tablet hooked up to Google Jam also works well.

You need to find the right tool that works best for you — one that is aligned with your organisation. There's probably no point scheduling a Google Hangout when the rest of the organisation uses Skype for Business, for example.

CO-CREATE YOUR USER PERSONAS

Creating some personas as a group is a great way to start a new piece of work. There are many different approaches to creating personas but here's the process I generally like to follow:

Step 1 – Qualitative personas research

Collate insights from initial user interviews, and then workshop some ideas with clients, co-workers and stakeholders to create a *proto-persona* (rough outline). This is your qualitative research and doesn't prove anything yet, so it's crucial to follow up with the next step.

Step 2 - Qualitative personas with quantitative validation

This might involve a survey and an analytics study such as site traffic data or other statistics that are available. Qualitative research with quantitative validation is about cross-checking your *proto-personas* with real data to create a more accurate insight.

I have included this simple persona workshop approach in my follow-up book, "Sweet Spot UX Workshops: Effective Design Facilitation for Perfect Business Alignment."

A CHANGE OF MINDSET

Whilst many UX designers said that common solutions they used involved educating their clients or stakeholders using data or user videos to back up their rationale, much of their frustration is actually deeply rooted in communication problems. For example, in order to overcome the UX pain point 'Ignorance, and unwillingness to listen, and a lack of understanding', you need to learn to educate your business — take them on the journey by aligning with them. In order to overcome the UX pain point 'Multi-directional project priorities that don't support UX', you need to sell the value of UX so that it earns a place in the competing project plan. And in order to break through the UX pain point 'Time constraints mean no budget for UX', you need to begin to prove how UX saves the business time and money — showing that the process of designing something is completely measurable and has a tangible ROI.

When I say communication, none of those things are solved simply by 'saying it'. Communication in the UX world involves a lot more 'doing' than 'saying'. That's why design workshops are so important — not just for design outcomes themselves, but for the evolving alignment that you gain over time between you and the others in your business.

To understand the 'We already know what the user wants' problem, first we have to establish empathy and detach ourselves from our own expertise for a second. No matter what the maturity of the organisation is, your co-workers and stakeholders are unlikely to be trained in the field of UX and so much of the terminology we use like 'Information Architecture', 'Heuristic Review', 'Ethnographic Study', or acronyms like 'UI' 'UCD' or 'IA' won't make a lot of sense to them.

What co-workers, stakeholders and clients do know about UX has likely come from who they've worked with before, what they've read, or what they've heard. Each of these may lead to totally different interpretations of what UX actually means. So instead of using our preferred terms, as UX designers we need to also learn to speak the language of the business we are in.

CHAPTER FIVE

MASTERING THE ART OF COMMUNICATION
FOR BEST RESULTS

"Any problem can be made clearer with a picture, and any picture can be created using the same set of tools and rules."

– Dan Roam[12]

This is the most important chapter of this book — and for good reason – design *is* communication. Mastering the process of communicating through design inside a business is more of an art than a science though. UX is becoming a very crowded space these days, and UX designers who lack business maturity to compete in the real world can easily get left behind. Some of the key skills that employers seek these days not only includes software skills, user research and proven design innovation, but they also seek UX designers who possess an ability to communicate and present their work effectively.

Whilst mastering good UX communication is critical to every UX designer's success, I believe that far too often it gets placed in the 'too-hard basket'. When this happens, UX designers fall into the trap of just being design implementers, which in turn can lead to frustration.

Watch out for these common signals:
- **Stakeholders making decisions on behalf of users**
  Even if they mean well, stakeholders are likely misinformed about what makes a good user experience, especially if they are not inside the heads of their customers.

---

[12] Roam, D. (2012). *The back of the napkin: Solving problems and selling ideas with pictures.* Marshall Cavendish International.

- **UX presentations used to discuss personal preferences**
  It's all too common to be drawn into discussions about subjective 'likes' and 'dislikes' with your stakeholders.
- **Assumptions used as business requirements**
  Too often, design assumptions are allowed to be converted straight into business requirements without being tested by users. This leads to prioritising features that are of low value and are not solving real user problems.

Clearly, not placing enough emphasis on communicating the value of UX is one of the most disastrous mistakes a UX designer can make. It can lead to ineffective design and an overall decay in the trust and credibility of UX within the organisation. A UX designer can then start to feel frustrated and may leave the organisation hoping to find something better, only to find the same issues exist elsewhere.

LEARNING TO BE A BETTER UX COMMUNICATOR

The difference between being a good communicator and a great communicator in UX is often just about mastering the art of storytelling and collaboration in equal parts. This means knowing *how* to get your point across in the right way to the right people and knowing *when* to kick off a whiteboard session or remote workshop to solve a problem or defuse a debate.

Being a good communicator is not just about having the 'gift of the gab'. That's useful, of course, but the number one critical skill of a good communicator in UX design is being a good listener. This means having empathy for those you are communicating to — really understanding their perspective and motivations, acknowledging that their opinions may be different to yours, being able to accept feedback (and sometimes criticism), being able to deliver a strong persuasive argument when needed, and also knowing when not to.

CHARISMA AND INFLUENCE

In any business situation, you will come across people who are difficult to deal with. But just because they are difficult doesn't mean you need to respond accordingly. If someone is being difficult, that's actually an indication that there is an opportunity there to try to understand their business perspective. Being argumentative by default means you're missing the opportunity to use charismatic influence to build a better relationship. You should try to respond to obstruction or criticism with politeness and curiosity, rather than becoming the "jerk no one can work with", to use the UX Australia quote from earlier.

So, just like when you have empathy for your users, you should also strive for the same level of empathy with your clients and stakeholders, and for others inside your organisation. That means using the same techniques that you would use in customer interviews: Ask lots of 'why' questions to dig deeper into understanding the real problem, rather than dictating a design solution to the business based on what you think is right.

In a user-testing session, you learn not to ask *leading* questions. For example, you would never say to a user, "Would you tap on this button?" Instead, you might say something like, "What would you do next on this screen?" to ascertain whether they would tap on the button, or what expectations they would have for tapping / not tapping on the button.

Taking this same open and unbiased approach with stakeholders is extremely useful. For example, when a client or stakeholder says to me, "I don't think that design is a good experience for our customers," I'd likely say, "I did it this way because of x, y and z," but I'd also say, "I'm really interested in what your thoughts are." By immediately empathising and expressing curiosity, I let them have their say and carefully acknowledge it before making any counter point.

In my response, rather than being defensive (my natural inclination because I am a sensitive designer), I accept it as an interesting point, but also as an assumption that still needs validating. If I have already validated my design, I will say so. If not, and it's an important point that I missed, I will also say so. I try to never dismiss an opinion nor argue it, but instead accept it as valid input, and a learning about the business perspective. Then I will ask if it's something we (as a group) think we should spend more time investigating, or if we think it's safe to proceed and monitor it later. Regardless, I will note it all carefully, reassure them that I will look into it, and make sure I come back with a response in due course. Then I move on.

I realise that is a huge oversimplification and assumes things always go to plan, which of course they don't. That's why this book doesn't end here; I will continue to share detailed insights I have learned from communicating to stakeholders and decision makers, including how to speak their language.

THE ART OF LISTENING

Business empathy is the path to understanding

If you can learn to understand your business, your trust and credibility will increase, which will enable you to do more UX work. Doing more UX work means adding more value to the lives of your customers. I've worked with a lot of UX designers over the years and, in my experience, I'd say many don't always strive for this business alignment. They are focused primarily on the user-side of their work and see the business they work for as an obstacle that needs to be overcome in order to create better experiences for their users.

Usually, when we start out in UX design, it's because we love the creative science of it, not because we want to find a profession that gets us into the world of business and politics. That's why many UX designers can sometimes struggle at the start of their careers to get their ideas out there and find it difficult to evangelise the value of user experience in their organisation. But the harsh reality is, if you're a UX designer who doesn't take the time to understand business and speak the language of the business in which you work, making the jump from a design implementer to a strategic UX leader will be a challenge.

The first step to overcome this challenge is a change of mindset. As UX designers, we are taught (or should be taught) about developing empathy for our users; that is, getting inside the heads of our users and really understanding their frustrations and pain points helps us design better products. Yet, when turning our focus back to the workplace, it's all too easy to complain about politics or frustrations we have with stakeholders who are not supporting our initiatives in the right way.

Whether we like it or not, the business and its stakeholders are our users too. In UX we sit in that sweet spot between customers and the business, so addressing the needs of the customer and the business simultaneously is key. In a way, we exist in a void — a vacuum between two worlds, where we strive to understand the customer whilst also solving the problem on behalf of the business we work for.

If you encounter a resistant stakeholder and ignore the opportunity to build a relationship with them, you will struggle to gain trust. Without trust, you will find it difficult to convince them to invest in more of your work.

THE 4 UX MINDSET PRINCIPLES

To make the jump from a deliverable-driven design role into a more strategic UX leadership role, there are four key mindset principles you should adopt. Solidify them into your team, your co-workers and the wider organisation.

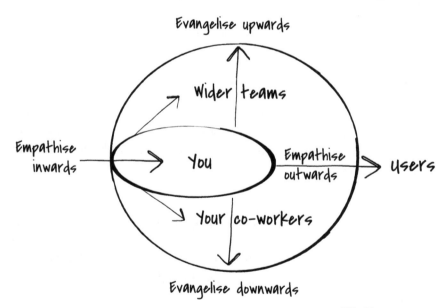

Mike Newman © 2021

1. Empathise outwards

Empathy for your users is integral to any UX role and should be the core of your UX mindset. To be a UX designer, you need to develop the ability to fully understand your users' needs and motivations. That empathy will allow you to understand your users' frustrations, but also their goals and expectations of your product.

2. Empathise inwards

Likewise, empathy for your business is also key. You should treat co-workers and stakeholders like your users. In effect, they *are* also your users by contributing an important aspect to the product and without your business needs, you would not have a product or users. So, empathy for your organisation means understanding your stakeholders' frustrations, goals and expectations of the product.

3. Evangelise upwards

Having captured your users' expectations, preferences and pain points, you need to become their voice within your organisation. You need to be skilled at mirroring and sharing your users' frustrations and expectations back to your business in a way they understand and can relate to. The empathy for your users' needs will start to resonate with the people around you.

4. Evangelise downwards

Lead by example on the above three principles for other members in your team or co-workers to follow — whether they are other designers, developers or something else, these principles should be reinforced by those around you.

Taking the responsibility of these principles means *clearing the path* for other UX designers in your team or organisation to succeed. As a UX leader, you should aim to set these principles in motion, have the hard conversations with stakeholders, and ensure that educating and evangelising becomes part of the culture.

On top of that you should try to establish a mentor-level leadership. Don't wait for someone to ask you to be their mentor; offer your mentorship to those in your team who are willing to learn and can benefit from your advice. This will give them the confidence they need to succeed in each of the above principles.

How to build empathy with your stakeholders

When starting a new project, the first thing a great UX designer should do is get to know their stakeholders — get inside their heads and understand the problems they want to solve. In doing so, you will comprehend the boundaries and constraints of their business world, building trust and finding out where the goal posts are. Sure, you can try to move the goal posts a bit later if required, but to begin with you need to show your stakeholders that you are on their team and can strike some goals.

Instead of showing frustration to a resistant stakeholder, take the time to see things from their perspective. Rather than seeing them as a difficult, anti-UX person who is blocking you from doing your job, treat them as a partner and as an opportunity to learn more about the 'business user' who also has needs and pain points. When discussing a problem or idea they have, be curious and be sure to ask why. You might not agree with their perspective, but you can at least acknowledge it and treat it as a user insight that will help you later.

In Chapter 3 I talked about conducting stakeholder safaris, but you could also conduct more guerrilla-style 'water cooler' conversations about a project you are working on, asking for their thoughts and advice on some design challenges you have. Be sure to show genuine curiosity and interest in what they say. When you get to know them more, propose an idea you have for how a piece of UX work might help them in a project you know is important to them.

If you're thinking that's all much easier said than done, you'd be right. You will always meet obstructive people in business who are just simply difficult and building empathy and understanding with them feels like bashing your head against a wall. These people may need a unique approach and there is a section later in this chapter that might help in dealing with just such difficult characters.

ACTIVITIES TO INCREASE YOUR BUSINESS EMPATHY

- Search for articles about the leaders of your organisation and try to understand what the organisation's success looks like for them.
- Study the organisation's strategic material, such as its larger organisational vision and business objectives, and any core values and principles for its employees. Then try to build them into your communications around UX for relevance and meaning.
- Ask to be involved in any strategy meetings to help learn more about the business and to help you design a product that is more in line with their business objectives.
- Create a presentation on how UX can add value, tailored to business leaders and executives.

THE ART OF SPEAKING

It's about being prepared and thinking ahead

Once you understand that getting inside your stakeholder's head is just as important as getting inside the heads of your users, you will start to understand the mindset of a sweet spot UX designer. But to take this a step further, you will also need to start making effective stakeholder communication part of your 'business as usual' activity. Here are a few tips:

Preparing for a presentation

- Make sure you know the outcomes you want to get from the meeting or presentation and be clear about communicating what you want. Is it a conceptual design session where you are open to brainstorming ideas, or are you after design feedback on a specific feature interaction?
- Know who you are speaking to and prepare your story accordingly. Make sure your story connects to the business goals or requirements and use language that is fitting to the audience. For example, a presentation to your immediate team may be very different to one to your stakeholders. If executives are attending, you should prepare an executive summary, so they don't need to attend the whole meeting if they aren't able to.

- Be prepared to adapt a presentation to fit with the different perspectives of each audience. This will allow them to identify with their areas of expertise. For example, if you are working on the user flow for a graduate application, you may want to consider a human resources perspective; or if it's a design that contains financial information, you may want your conversation to fit with an accounting or legal audience. Conduct a dry-run with a co-worker to check timings, pick up any errors and make sure your message is clear and easy for your audience to understand.

Conducting a presentation

Present your story at a high-level first, clearly and concisely, and delve into details later as needed.

- During discussions, constantly remind colleagues of what you are doing and why. Clearly articulate the problem you are trying to solve, the outcomes you want to achieve, and the process you intend to adopt to achieve it.
- Try to steer conversations away from personal preferences by leading them back to the problem you are trying to solve and the business goal.
- Be open to feedback — recognise that it's not just designers who have valid input. Feedback or comments from non-designers is an opportunity to delve more into the underlying need or question from the business, so give them the opportunity to talk and ask questions. Remain empathetic even when you disagree, as this helps uncover unexpected issues.
- Actively confirm by translating and playing back your discussions to the group to check your understanding is correct. For example, say, "So, this is what I'm hearing, is that correct?" Guide them to elaborate, to clarify any confusion and make notes, then let them know you will need some time to think about it.
- Remember, it's okay to take time out to respond. As UX designers we often feel we should know all the answers right away, but if you encounter something you don't know the answer to, it's okay to ask for an opinion and take some time to assess and respond later.

- Manage your tone and inflection. It's easy to be sensitive to feedback — we've all been there — but be careful not to respond in an emotional way. Remain curious and interested in what people say even when the feedback could be interpreted as a criticism of your work. Recognise that *most* people who give feedback also want to design a better product.

After the presentation

- Make sure you set aside time to review the notes you made during the presentation (or play back your recording). Take the time to consider each piece of feedback before you decide whether to do something with it.
- Use follow-up communication to confirm what was discussed and to clarify any confusion. Remind everyone what was agreed upon and what the next steps are and consider if you need to highlight anything specific to co-workers who weren't in the meeting.
- Consider if you need to address anything directly with an individual. This allows you to have a more direct conversation with the person who provided the feedback but remember to communicate the outcomes with everyone else that was in attendance later.
- If you have a documentation process in place (such as a Wiki) take the time to write it up so you don't lose track later.

DESIGNING AS A TEAM

Try to hold the team accountable for your designs too. Involve them early in the design process, capture as much input as you can and relay it back to them when you present your idea. Addressing your audience with the words *we* and *our* instead of *I* and *my* also helps to establish a sense of group accountability.

For example, I often start by recapping what we've done to date by saying, "We discussed this, then we went away and did some user research, and our resulting concept looks like this." Or by saying, "This is the initial design concept based on our recent discussions, I would like to get your feedback so we can figure out what's working and what we need to change or re-test with our users."

THE ART OF A PERFECT UX MINDSET

Learn how to back yourself

As I mentioned earlier in this book, defending design decisions takes practice, and to be successful requires a change in mindset, leading you away from being argumentative about an opinion but also being assertive enough to articulate your point of view.

To achieve all this takes practice — it took me years — from the moment in my hero's journey when I realised I needed to overcome my tenuous sense of legitimacy, to today where I'm writing this book and running workshops in my sleep. But I am still learning and growing. Whilst it takes practice no matter where you are in your career, I have a collated a few tips that will help give you an edge.

You are *not* your design. It's true you may have put a lot into it, and you might be really happy with the outcome and believe it's the right solution to the problem. But it's not just you critiquing your work; and even the best designs won't always be received with open arms.

Don't be the sensitive designer

This can be a problem for all of us in a profession where our work is constantly critiqued and judged. It's extremely hard to remove yourself from any personal attachment you have to an idea or design. It's very easy to take things to heart and feel like criticisms of your work are somehow a reflection on your ability as a designer, or that the person giving the critique is aiming at you rather than the design.

As a result, getting something approved can feel like an uphill struggle. And in many cases, it's not just one person from whom you might face resistance, it could be across multiple people or entire teams. For example, a developer could be resistant to change because change means more work, a product manager may have issues with your design that are based on some key business requirements that aren't in line with user needs or goals, or an executive may have a personal opinion that they wish to have upheld because they are seen as the key decision maker in the process.

These obstructions can be frustrating and, if you take them personally, it's easy to feel offended. But it's important to remember that these are just feelings and emotions. They are natural but not necessary in making an informed decision about a design. Being a strong UX designer means learning to leave your feelings behind, and instead aim for aligning everybody towards the same goal. Read on, and I will provide some more tips on how to do that.

You are not the only designer in the room

These days, the reality is that UX design is rarely the responsibility of *just* the UX designer. To be successful, you have to shift your mindset to a more holistic view of designing. Design shouldn't be a solitary activity — the job of an expert who knows best — it should be the job of the collective expertise around you.

So, part of the perfect UX mindset is recognising that you're not solely responsible for solving all the design problems. It's not you against them; it's all of you together designing for the benefit of the user. Whether you like it or not, the developers, project managers, managers, senior managers and clients are contributing to and influencing the end product that you're designing, so in fact they are designers too. Obviously, they are unlikely to be getting on the tools and designing a user interface in Sketch, or using Smaply to draw out a user journey, but they can easily help you sketch out those ideas on paper or on a screen, and in doing so they will be influencing the end-product and the user experience in a positive way.

Overcoming a fear of presenting

Some people seem to be natural presenters and standing up in front of complete strangers with a Steve Jobs swagger seems to come easily for them. If you're one of those people, then good for you! But for the vast majority of us, it doesn't come naturally and takes both hard work and practice before it becomes easier. I remember at university we all had to stand up in front of the whole year and present a piece of design work, and most people were, excuse my French, shitting themselves. Some of my colleagues nailed it their first time, but many others stuttered, mumbled and went bright red. Some couldn't speak at all, one person ran out of the room, and at least two people were conveniently off sick that day.

In my experience, even at an advanced stage of my career, presenting something can flip between easy and challenging depending on what it is, how comfortable I am with the audience, and how much I know about the content I am presenting. Presenting becomes more challenging when you step out of your comfort zone. For example, when I first stood up and spoke about the upcoming release of this book to other authors and potential critics, I was nervous. But the thing about your comfort zone is, staying in it doesn't help, and each time you step outside, you learn something and grow.

I realised that a large part of my speech wasn't resonating with the audience, who didn't really understand what UX was, which was the whole purpose of the book. A lot of the time I was speaking directly to other UX designers of whom there were only a handful in the room — mainly those I had invited myself. I felt embarrassed when I saw blank faces looking back at me, but I learned a lot for next time. When presenting this book to an audience, I need know who they are and tailor the story for them.

Why does a fear of presenting exist?

They say that a fear of presenting comes from your mind and your past experiences. The oldest part of our brain —referred to as the reptilian brain — controls our basic motor functions, including those for survival. If we had to think consciously about breathing and digestion, we wouldn't get very far.

We also have a built-in survival mechanism that kicks in when our 'instinct' feels we are in danger. This is often referred to as the fight or flight response. This response produces a chemical reaction that prepares our bodies to fight or to take flight. When this chemical response occurs, it interferes with our physiology — our heart rate in particular — but it also affects our brains and can easily cloud our judgement and ability to think straight.

So, when you are standing up prepping to present for the first time, your body thinks you are in danger and in a way, instead of feeling relaxed and accepted, you actually feel like you are standing up preparing to fight the crowd of people in front of you. And in the back of your mind somewhere there might even be a little voice telling you to run away. "I can't do this, why am I here? Maybe I should go?" it says. Like my university colleagues who literally ran out of the room before their big presentation.

The problem too is that when you have a bad experience of presenting, it can make things worse. You start to dwell on the fear of presenting rather than focusing on delivering a kick-ass presentation and after a while, this fear, if not overcome, can sink into your subconscious and stop you from ever wanting to leave your comfort zone. Earlier in this book, I discussed my own hero's journey and getting mocked when accepting an award for art during a school assembly. The fear of this happening again meant I began to avoid centre stage, often without even realising it; the fear had moved to my subconscious.

In my early years as a designer, I remember telling myself that I didn't need to present to big audiences or do huge talks in front of people to be a good designer; someone else could always do that stuff for me. I should be able to focus just on what I'm good at, which I thought was design. The fear of rejection and humiliation are very powerful forces that can often prevent us from achieving our full potential and, in the case of UX design, can end up being a huge obstacle.

Generally, the way to overcome this is to first change your mindset, then do it over and over again until it becomes a habit. Like my friend who lacked confidence in presentations — after working for a top New York agency where she had to do it every day, she suddenly got very good at it and is now a confident presenter.

Finally, know that it's okay to fail, and it's okay to say to people, "Sorry if I wasn't at my best, I'm still learning and growing."

Here are a few tips for developing the right mindset for presenting:

#1
DITCH THE "TED TALK PERFORMER" MINDSET

The best approach for overcoming a fear of presenting is to change your perspective from that of a 'performer' to a 'communicator'. Remember, you are not there to deliver the world's best TED Talk (maybe save that for another day), you are simply there to achieve your immediate goal of getting your point across in the right way, to the right people in the room. The mistake I made early in my career was to continually compare myself to others and think, "I wish I presented as well as them," which in turn led to a feeling of insecurity, which led to a fear of not being good enough.

What I have learnt since, is that presenting is just a form of communication. Instead of presenting on stage to an audience, you are just communicating to a room your idea, your challenge, or your solution. So rather than getting caught up on whether people are judging you on the way you present, try to adjust your thinking towards achieving the immediate goal of communicating something successfully to them.

This approach will then help free you from the pressure of perfection and allow you to make mistakes on your journey of communicating the value of UX within your business. If you have ever had a presentation that didn't resonate, it's easy to beat yourself up over it, but next time try a different way of communicating your idea to that type of audience and keep experimenting with it until you find a style that fits with you and that works with them. Over time you will be able to more easily adapt your presentations to fit the types of audiences you are speaking to. Your presentation mindset should always be a work in progress.

#2
DRY-RUN IT, EVEN IF IT'S ON YOUR OWN

Rehearsing gives you confidence, even if it's only to be able to tell yourself, "It's okay, I got this, I've rehearsed it, I know it." This approach doesn't work with everyone though. It definitely helps me, but I also find that if I *over-rehearse* I start to *over-think* it and then I start to waste time seeking unnecessary perfection. What works for me is to find a trusted colleague to run it past once or twice beforehand. That way I can iron out any of the little mistakes and have the confidence to know I have cleaned it up and received feedback ahead of the session. Like any design feedback, remember not to be too sensitive to suggested alterations.

For bigger, more important presentations where a higher level of perfection is required, I try to rehearse them out loud on my own — recording them on my phone so I can play them back. The first time you do this can be a little confronting, and it is tempting to skip over this step, but it does help build confidence when you work through it and adjust any little quirks you notice in your presentation style.

#3
PRACTISE VISUALISATION

Visualising success is a technique used by athletes, and it works because you are filling yourself with positive beliefs, telling your brain that the event you are going to do is not a threat, and therefore doesn't require a fight or flight response.

The idea is to simply run through it in your mind and visualise how a calm confident presentation would come across to those you are presenting. I find with this, it also helps to know where you are presenting and to how many people if you can, so as to more accurately visualise what the real presentation will be like on the day. The good thing about this technique is you can do it anywhere — lying in bed, sitting on the bus, walking in the park.

#4
EVEN IF YOU'RE NOT FEELING CONFIDENT, PRETEND YOU ARE

UX designers love statistics and human psychology. We love observing how our users behave when using one of our products and analysing the data to find the "Ah-ha" moment. But it's also true that, as humans, we too are subject to the same rules of human behaviour as our users. Even when presenting a great piece of UX design, we can easily find ourselves frustrated when confronted with a difficult audience and lose confidence in ourselves when they don't respond in the way we expected.

You may have heard this before: According to Albert Mehrabian, professor of psychology from the University of California in the 1960s, only 7% of communication contains words. The other 93% is non-verbal, being made up of body language (55%) and tone of voice (38%).[13] Obviously, body language and tone of voice are important when presenting. And the clear benefit in knowing about body language is that if you practice, you will eventually feel more confident and relaxed about presenting. The other aspect of body language is to combine it with the right tone of voice to influence people and learning how to put them at ease. When you can put others at ease, it also puts you at ease, which links back to the first point about body language giving you confidence.

---

[13] Mehrabian, A. (2017). *Nonverbal communication.* [ePub]. Routledge.

#5
USE YOUR BODY LANGUAGE

There has been a lot written about body language and presenting, and it's probably worth reading them to get the full value. But the key thing to remember about it is that it's mostly just acting. It's been proven that projecting confident body movements can actually make you more confident. Of course, this doesn't necessarily affect how people will receive you. A difficult person in the room may still be difficult, but improvements to your body language will at least make you feel better about yourself.

Here are some guidelines on how body language and posture can help you to project confidence during a presentation:[14]

Keep your chin up

You'll notice in a sport like soccer or tennis that when a professional sportsperson's confidence drops, you often see their head go down. Try to keep your head and chin up regardless of how you feel, as this is a key indicator of confidence versus nerves.

Uncross your arms

Having your arms crossed can be a habit for some people, but this sets a defensive, 'closed-in' stance and makes others adopt a more defensive and 'closed-in' attitude to mirror yours. Watch carefully what happens when you cross your arms when talking to someone, compared to uncrossing them.

Face your audience

Subconsciously, your body position points to where your mind wants to go. If you keep turning your body towards the door during a meeting or presentation, it's a subtle sign that you don't want to be there. Instead, make sure you turn square on to your audience.

---

[14] Some of these tips were interpreted from Wrighton, T. (2013) *The secrets of body language in 30 minutes*. [Audiobook]. Puttenham Ltd.

Avoid fidgeting

Fidgeting comes across as being nervous, whereas being still exudes strength and confidence. Nervous energy can create tension, which can be easily transferred to others in the room, creating once again a 'closed-in' attitude with your audience. If you are inclined to fidget during a presentation, try standing still but keeping your arms in front of you in an open manner and use your hands to help explain the points in your presentation. This takes practise and it might also help to video record yourself to refine your technique.

#6
PUT OTHERS AT EASE

Here are some pointers on how to use body language and tone to put others at ease:

Be open

Keep your posture as open as possible when presenting. Make sure your arms (and legs if you are seated) are uncrossed. An open posture helps create an open attitude.

Encourage them to be open

When people are defensive, they often cross their arms; whereas when their arms are open, they are more likely to be receptive to you. This is one of the reasons why workshop activities are so valuable — getting your audience to do an open activity, rather than sitting in a closed-off position for the whole presentation, is really helpful. This helps break down any inflexible points of view.

Choose your words and tone carefully

The words and tone you use can support the desired influence of your body language and help compel your audience to be more attuned and open to your presentation. For example, using positive affirmations to your audience like, "Isn't it awesome?" and, "Imagine how good that would be?" sets the mood and the mindset of your audience.

Smile

This is not always easy if you are feeling nervous, but a smile can ease the tension in the room. I know many good presenters who incorporate some light humour or include a small light-hearted activity at the start of their session, to help soften the mood and create some smiles.

Mirroring

This one is better suited for one-on-one or small group presentations. People like people who mimic them, and all the best communicators are masters of this technique, whether they realise it or not. For example, if you lean back in your chair, they do too. If you touch your face, they do too. Mirroring is not about being creepy, or a body language hack, it's about aligning your body language with theirs — because aligning yourself with them helps create a connection, and a sense of alignment in your frame of mind.

THE ART OF DEALING WITH DIFFICULT PEOPLE

Defending design decisions without defending design decisions

As a UX designer, you will experience many scenarios where you feel unprepared for an onslaught of obstructive criticism of your work; and if you are not prepared for this, it can mean enduring a lot of frustration. Perhaps you invested a lot of effort into a design solution but got caught off-guard when it came under fire. Perhaps you didn't have enough reliable evidence to defend your design decision, or perhaps you got overruled by the HiPPO in the room who already had a solution in mind, and you ended up adopting the "uselessly agreeable" persona and leaving with your tail between your legs.

This happened to me many times early on in my career, and I know it's a tough pill to swallow. Just because you're confident in your proposed design solution to solve a problem for customers doesn't mean other people are necessarily going to agree with you.

YOU DON'T HAVE TO HAVE ALL THE ANSWERS

It's okay to acknowledge that you don't know the answer, and you need time to assess. Remember, you aren't meant to be able to solve all of the problems for your customers, but you are on the journey with them to solve all of their problems. Being upfront about that helps create a sense of openness about your work and being open for feedback often means you lead people more into discussions, rather than debates and arguments.

TIP: Try to turn it back on them by finding out more about what they are trying to achieve. Explain that your expertise isn't just about giving off-the-cuff answers without knowing more about their goals. Try to understand the problem and then take some time to be able to properly advise.

So, how do you defend design decisions without defending design decisions? Here are some communication techniques that I (and other experienced UX designers) commonly use:

Learn to anticipate the arguments

It usually helps if you can address issues up-front rather than waiting to defend yourself. So before presenting anything to a difficult stakeholder, it often helps to take a step back from your work and view it from an outsider's perspective. Running through a design with a trusted colleague can help view it more objectively, and help you identify any issues you might encounter in your meeting. Once you can identify the aspects of your design that might receive criticism, you can start to formulate a strategy for how you might respond.

There's a great scene in the film *8 Mile*, starring Eminem, where Jimmy faces off his opponent Papa Doc in a rap battle. Everyone expected him to lose against his most feared rival, but Jimmy won the battle because he anticipated exactly what his opponent was going to say about him — and said it all first. With nothing left to say, Papa Doc dropped the mic and quit.

Similarly, when faced with a difficult character in a meeting, a good way to address critical questions is to pre-empt them and answer them first. In many cases, you may already know what a difficult person might ask you, so address it head on as part of your presentation, rather than wait to defend it.

For example, if you anticipate a key stakeholder will try to debunk your testing methods by saying, "Why did you only test with five people?" make sure you have a slide in your deck that refers to the reason why we test with five people, perhaps citing a well-known UX thought leader like Jakob Nielsen. This is much better explained upfront as part of the process, rather than responding to it later under duress.

Turn the focus back on them

It's very easy to tell you to anticipate the arguments, but of course in reality you cannot anticipate everything. You don't want to spend all your time trying to do that and not have any time left to design anything. For example, a stakeholder may, out of the blue, request a completely different feature or suggests changing the layout or colour of a button to improve the user experience. These suggestions often are unsubstantiated and based purely on a subjective point of view, but sometimes they may be valid points and worthy of consideration, so show interest and ask questions to try to understand "why" it is important to them.

I remember once being put on the spot in a meeting where I'd incorporated a particular interface element for an app. It wasn't the best solution, but it worked for what we were trying to do within the scope of the project and was technically feasible. In that meeting, I was cornered by the difficult character who asked, "How do you think using this improves the user experience of the app?" I gave a weak answer. This was quickly followed by, "I read an article by Jakob Nielsen who said that is a bad user experience, so I was just wondering why you chose it." What I felt at the time was a sense of failure — I should have prepared the perfect answer for this, a rationale for why I had designed it that way. In the context of this specific case, it made sense and was a good solution, but I wasn't prepared for the question, and so my instinct led to a poor rationale.

I now know that my expertise shouldn't be based on giving off-the-cuff answers without knowing more about what they want to achieve; it should be based on understanding the problem and advising accordingly. So, here are some ways in which I could have responded:

"It's a great topic to discuss, and there's a lot of debate about the proper use of that in the UX industry. I'd really love to read that article and discuss it more."

"So why are you asking about it? What are your thoughts and what did you have in mind?"

"I thought it'd work well for this scenario, but we could definitely look at alternatives too if we think it's important to spend more time on it. I'll schedule some time after this to discuss next steps with the team."

There's a whole range of ways you could structure the conversation into group problem-solving, rather than hero-design solutions, but the key point here is to remain curious and turn that curiosity back on them, showing empathy and interest in finding out more about what they want to achieve.

And if you do stumble on something like that, don't worry — we are all human. After you encounter a difficult comment or situation, you are always much more capable of responding to it again in the future, because now you can anticipate it.

Defer the discussion until later

Sometimes it's easy to get caught up in pointless debates — discussions that seem to continually go around and around in circles. These types of conversations are not always negative; sometimes they can be fun and feel like you're exchanging ideas, but the key thing is to recognise when something isn't actually going anywhere. As a UX facilitator, it is your job to recognise a rabbit-hole and move the conversation along, deferring the discussion for another time.

If the conversation is going nowhere, simply say something like, "This is a great discussion, but I don't think we are going to solve the whole problem today. Let's park it for now and come back another time," and then you can direct the conversation onto another topic. This technique buys you some time so you can solve the problem later without feeling like you're being forced to make decisions on the fly.

Focus on your best communication skill – design

It can help to supplement the conversation with visual aids. As designers, we are often much better equipped to talk about a design or a sketched concept than we are sitting around a table having a debate. Sharing a picture to articulate meaning or getting up and quickly sketching something on the whiteboard, takes the immediate focus off a debate about your design, and into a group discussion about the problem you are all trying to solve together. There will be many languages used in a group discussion: the language of the developer who is speaking functionality, the language of the project manager who is speaking timelines and budgets, and the language of the visual designer who is speaking look and feel. All of these can easily be translated into a shared understanding with the use of a simple sketch to clarify meaning and align thinking.

Having a discussion over a whiteboard or a screen-share during a conference call is usually much more effective than presenting a stuffy slideshow of spec'd up wireframes. The use of the whiteboard or sketching should be done as early in the discussion as possible. I have often gone to people's desks with a pad of paper and a pencil if needed or organised a quick Jam session over Google Hangouts to clarify a point in pictures when working remotely.

This approach saves a lot of time spent on designs and prototypes that end up getting reworked over and over due to a lack of understanding. When everyone is on the same page, and you need customer feedback; that's the time to get into the tools and prototype your design more carefully.

Arm yourself with data

As a UX designer, you are likely to have a plethora of user research at your disposal to support your design decisions. It might seem obvious, but ensuring you have this data with you, and ready to present in context of your design, is critically important for communicating what you are trying to achieve and garner support.

If you are designing a shopping cart for an ecommerce product, for example, the numbers will speak for themselves. Here you can talk about conversion metrics and cart abandonment rates. But the approach should be applicable to all designs in some way. There's always some user data to support how your design decision provides a solution.

It is most beneficial to present such data at the start of each new project, feature, or user story to provide perspective for your designs to follow. For example, before designing anything, you could dissect user feedback from your app or website into a compelling customer journey to help align everyone around the personas you are designing for. Without a discovery insight, it is easy for non-UX designers to get lost in the world of just trying to create solutions. In one organisation I worked in, I was asked to redesign the 'contact us' page on the main website and a key requirement was to remove the phone number. The intent was to force customers into a self-service contact form because it was better for the business. It was driven by an underlying business goal of reducing calls to the service centre. But making the phone number hard to find, whilst successful from a business goal standpoint, would certainly have had a fundamental knock-on effect to the experience for customers who were genuinely seeking to call. It would lead to frustration and bad sentiment, which would then affect customer satisfaction and other things like the business' overall Net Promoter Score (NPS). In this situation, it was tempting to be "uselessly agreeable" and go along with it, or to go to the other extreme and argue in total disagreement. The best approach in this scenario is to understand the requirement and its purpose, and to reflect on that alongside the customer perspective and purpose. In this case, I collected what I could to help paint a picture using data collected from various sources including visual analytics, feedback from previous user testing, existing website feedback, and industry statistics about self-service. This data helped frame the problem that needed to be solved for the business and the user. A design workshop was conducted where the business decision makers could then help steer design suggestions to solve 'user problems' as well as addressing the overarching 'business goal'.

Generally speaking, there is nothing more powerful than designing with data. Analytics of a page showing why important features should be moved or removed is a powerful way to support any design decision. Watching a video of a user being interviewed about that specific change can also be extremely compelling and helps articulate it in context with empathy for real users.

You can also refer to data gleaned from industry research or expert articles to support your position. Or, if you have previously established some base design principles that are tried and tested (more on that later), you can also use these to strengthen your point of view ahead of testing.

Provide the illusion of choice

OK, choice isn't really an illusion, it's just choice. But choice can be a very powerful way to manage a design debate with a difficult client or stakeholder. Why? Well, consider this: Proposing a single design is essentially about selling *that* design to your client or stakeholder, whereas presenting a choice changes your sales pitch into a conversation, moving it away from their (and your) personal opinions on the design towards a combined choice of which design is better and why.

In my early career I worked a lot for design agencies, and we used "choice" to help guide clients to settle on a design without getting too side-tracked by non-specific and subjective ideas. We would present three design concepts to give them the illusion of choice, but one was a real winner; the other two were left-field ideas unlikely to be chosen. It may sound misleading, but the intention was to illustrate why the primary concept was better, by comparing it to the other two: "We are recommending this one because, as you can see, it's better in these areas." What would often happen is the client would pick the recommended one, suggest some changes be brought across from the other two, then they would sign off with no further changes.

In the UX world, it's a bit different. What I often tend to do is provide two perfectly valid solutions, both of which I would be comfortable with. We then have the conversation about the pros and cons of both, let them pull both options apart, then I would re-construct them in a collaborative design session. I would then present a 'final' skew; one you already know your stakeholder will approve of, because it's had their input and buy-in. This is then the prototype for testing. There are of course other ways you could do this to a similar effect.

It's important to keep all of your previous iterations handy. In coming up with your preferred design, it's likely that you went through a number of different options, many of which you rejected for good reason. Be sure to keep all of these to hand so if you need to justify a choice to your client or stakeholder, you can present a previous iteration and explain how you went from that to your current design. Your goal here should be to present your preferred option by comparing it to one or two previous alternatives highlighting the reasons why they didn't work and are not as fit-for-purpose as the one you chose. But of course, remain open as you may not be right either.

Get them excited about something

Figure out what gets them excited. Perhaps it is Google Analytics data. Or a user recording providing some compelling feedback, or even a customer journey map or site architecture diagram. Whatever it is that resonates, find it, bring it, and capitalise on it.

Sometimes the smallest things can instigate a big mind shift. Recently, when I showed a stakeholder a demo of a visual analytics tool that enabled them to see heat maps of key pages and user sessions of what customers were doing on their product, they said, "Wow! How good is it to be able to see exactly what our customers are doing and how they are using it!" After that, I got approval for the software and was asked to do a presentation about it to the wider team. This led to more opportunities to sell the value of the team's great design capability elsewhere within the organisation.

Create a culture of co-designing

You can't always be right. If you were, you wouldn't be human and, as an advocate for human experiences, I'd say you're entitled to be wrong every now and then. For that reason, you should remember to give all debates and discussions due consideration and aim to build a rapport with your team so that you can have open and honest dialogue about design, rather than adopting a position of having to be right. No UX designer can live with that weight on their shoulders for long.

By using collaborative design techniques (covered in this book and in more detail in my next book), you will find that you achieve a much higher level of buy-in for your work. As time goes on, you will start to build a culture of UX co-designing around you, leading to much better experiences for you and your users, and will ultimately result in better support for your UX work in the future from those in your team.

This follows on from the previous point about the importance of designing as a team. When you foster a co-design mentality, you are also building a support network. Having UX advocates who understand the UX design process and the reason behind your solution, will help when dealing with the pushy stakeholder who wants to influence your work based on their own preference or agenda.

Build a support network

Defending a design decision is much easier when you have people in the room who will support your idea or solution. By building your support around you one-by-one, you will find that dealing with difficult stakeholders or clients becomes a lot easier.

In fact, if you've got the right people on your team, many of them might even do the defending without you. It helps if you have support from different areas of the business that cater to a broader perspective but who are all respectful of the UX work you are doing. For example, a developer, a product owner, a business analyst, a data analyst; whoever it is, if they are on your team, you are much better off.

For this to happen, you need to have already sold them the value of UX. If members of your team are uneducated in the ways of UX, or misinformed about what it is, then being able to explain it to them is crucial. I dedicate the next chapter to how to communicate UX to non-UXers.

CHAPTER SIX

COMMUNICATING UX TO NON UX PEOPLE

Designing anything of value always involves understanding other people, their needs and their perspectives.

> *"Human-centred design is a design philosophy. It means starting with a good understanding of people and the needs that the design is intended to meet."*
>
> – Donald Norman [15]

How many times have you been asked at a barbecue or dinner party, "So what do you do exactly?" Even for an experienced UX professional it can be a challenge to articulate the answer and, as soon as you do, the person seems to already have an opinion on what a good user experience is. I wish I had a dollar for every time a stranger said, "Oh so you're a web designer", and another dollar for, "Oh, that's I.T. right?" And if you try to talk about Customer Experience (CX), you'll likely face the comment, "Oh, you mean customer service?"

But aside from the challenge of describing what you do to family and friends, it's even more frustrating when your client or stakeholder believes they are experts in what makes a good user experience — an assumption-fuelled opinion disguised as a business requirement — one that is based purely on their own subjective viewpoint. Ten years ago, describing UX was much simpler. The landscape of design has changed so much, and the notion of the user experience is so ingrained in business and other disciplines that it has become a more complex and multi-disciplinary practice than it used to be, and it's much harder to categorise as a single thing.

---

[15] Norman, D. (2013). *The design of everyday things* (revised and expanded edition). [Kindle]. Basic Books.

The other factor is that UX design is rarely the responsibility of just the UX designer anymore. Because so many factors contribute to the overall experience of what you're designing for, UX has become the responsibility of whole teams — whether they realise it or not. Groups of people who are working together on a project are in fact all contributing to and influencing the end product that you're designing for. Whether it's designers, developers, project managers, managers, senior managers, or clients; all these people are UX designers, but each with a different perspective.

Unfortunately, each different perspective also brings a different dialect. Perhaps each member of the team uses the same words but, with their own subtly different language and intent, this can lead to confusion, frustration and misinterpretation. That's why communication is a critically important part of UX, and the first step is to communicate a consistent message of what UX is, initially to your immediate team, and then later to the rest of your business.

Communicating UX to your immediate team

In my experience, there is no exact science. Each business is different, and each team member has a different level of maturity in their understanding of UX practice. I've worked for many businesses and, in teams that are very immature in their understanding of what user experience is, I have had to literally start from scratch explaining its value, and trying to sell its worth to gain buy-in. I have also worked in teams that are quite mature in their understanding of user experience, but this often leads to them being inflexible to adopt different ways of doing things, sometimes to the detriment of the product experience.

SPEAKING IN LAYMAN'S TERMS

You can describe the basics of UX in layman's terms without patronising your audience or insulting their intelligence. For example, when describing the difference between UX and UI, simply say something along the lines of, "I am aware that many of you may already know this information, but I am describing it for clarity and consistency of meaning."

I worked in the digital marketing team of a business where the perception of user experience for many on the team was that it was about designing mock-ups for web pages and banners, while others thought it was just for instructing I.T. on what to build using wireframes. I also worked in the I.T. department of a large organisation where they were so ingrained in the 'what' of quantitative analytics that they had no desire in answering the 'why' with much-needed qualitative user research.

In each case the answer for me lay in gradually drawing the people around me into the real world of UX by taking them on a journey and involving them in the process at every step. I also took the time to expertly educate them with some well-timed "What is UX?" presentations. It doesn't need to be a dedicated 1-hour presentation where you try to re-educate the masses and turn them into advocates of your process. You *could* try that, and it works for certain audiences, but another way is to simply have a selection of key slides handy that you can add to an existing presentation to help your team, your stakeholders or clients. This could be slides about your user testing process when presenting a design solution to your team or slides to help articulate the difference between UX and UI when presenting a new feature concept to your stakeholders, for example.

In my next book, I will go into more detail about some practical topics and definitions that you can pick and choose from for your own "What is UX" presentation. I frequently use these as a reference to plug into my presentations and I supplement them with key messages to help educate and influence the perception of user experience with my team.

Communicating the value of UX to your wider team

Once you're comfortable that your immediate team are on-board with the value of your UX work, you need to start evangelising your message outwards to your stakeholders, especially any key decision makers. Of course, you could do both audiences simultaneously, but I find there is an advantage in refining your message with your co-workers first. I often use a 'UX Roadshow' format which consists of scheduling a presentation to key personnel as an information session about UX. You cover the basics of what UX means to your team or organisation, how it relates to them and how to get in touch if they would like more information or assistance. This works well, particularly if you have the support of your team and more importantly, your manager, who can advocate your message.

You can choose which topics to use depending on the level of business maturity of your audience and the context of your presentation. When doing so, the key thing to remember is to make sure your presentation has a story to tell. Be careful not to bore them; you need to 'theme' it and tailor the message to the organisation, ideally relating it to their overall vision or values.

For more details about suitable topics, see the next chapter where I go into more detail with specific tips and slide concepts.

Socialise your work

There is great value in socialising your UX work amongst your immediate and extended teams for visibility and credibility. It could involve anything from creating a Wiki page-like confluence or a dedicated research tool like Reframer, or utilising wall space in your office. I have found many organisations will encourage you to use a prominent wall space to promote work, and you can use it to communicate what you do to anyone who's interested, either by including your name and contact details or by inviting people to offer their opinion on a design or problem.

And of course, on top of everything else, you should just get out there and showcase your work to whoever will listen to a presentation. (See previous section about the art of communicating UX to non UXers.) Remember that the best tool to use is the one that gels the most with your team.

THE ART OF COLLABORATION AS A FORM OF COMMUNICATION

I think it's fair to say that these days the difference between a good designer and an excellent designer is based on their design facilitation skills. While a good designer can 'do good design', an excellent designer can also facilitate good design amongst a group of other, potentially non-designers. And there is nothing that can prepare you more for design leadership roles in the future like learning the art of facilitating design workshops.

To become a good facilitator, you need to learn the art of workshopping — the ability to set up and run a kick-ass workshop where you can guide team members and stakeholders through your UX design process. There are many problems a UX designer could encounter on this journey to workshopping mastery; for instance, you may have to negotiate your way through some resistance, including people who are just not interested in UX, much less want to participate in it. And even if you do have a room full of people who seem to get it, keeping their attention away from their phones, managing side-discussions, and coordinating everything on a schedule can be tricky. Even more so now as we all shift more into a remote-workshopping culture.

However, once you start to conduct design facilitation sessions properly, you'll learn how to quickly develop a shared understanding of your product and your team's intent. You will also find greater support in getting things done, but more importantly you'll have a much richer output of design innovation and better overall completeness; a solution that is backed by the diversity of differing professional backgrounds and disciplines of your team.

Being an excellent design facilitator is not only possible for a specific personality type either. Anyone can successfully run a design workshop. The only prerequisite is the desire to get people on-board with your design process and a willingness to make mistakes and adapt your style along the way. In my experience, there are many techniques and structures out there you can use for design workshops, but there is no real one-size-fits-all for every organisation. In every place I have worked, I have always had to adapt what I had created before to fit the unique culture of the new organisation. Your primary focus of any UX workshop should simply be to help guide the team through solving problems using a design process. If you can master the art of ad-hoc facilitation (such as getting up to whiteboard an idea, or quickly scheduling an online Jam session to clarify a problem), you will be seen more as a strategic designer and less of a design implementer. This will in turn help you achieve greater influence in your organisation and gaining support for your work will start to get much easier.

Planning your workshop should start by knowing what your outcome should be and there are plenty of resources out there that can help you plan and organise that. Whatever structure you use, you also need a willingness to experiment with it until you find the sweet spot of what works for your organisation.

GETTING STARTED:
START SMALL AND BUILD UP

If you're new to facilitating workshops, or feel you lack confidence, start small. In fact, even if you are experienced, but you're in a new organisation, my advice is to start small as well. This way you can learn and adapt your style to fit the business culture around you. Starting small might mean running a whiteboard brainstorming session with one or two design colleagues, then extending it to some cross-functional team members.

There are many formats and techniques that you can use: discovery workshops, empathy mapping, ideation workshops, prioritisation workshops; the list goes on. I'm not going to detail all of these in this book as there are already several guides and courses available. But I will highlight a few simple workshop examples that I often use to create a shared understanding, which in turn helps create a better focus on your users, leading to better support for your work.

Remote workshopping skills are a must

Sure, running a workshop in person where you can get your hands dirty with butcher's paper, post-it notes and sharpies is definitely more fun, and you can manage the room better, that's a given. However, these days that's becoming less frequent as more designers find themselves working with remote teams. Therefore, I believe mastering remote workshop skills are just as important for your future.

What I've learnt is that running a workshop remotely usually needs to be short and snappy as attention spans and concentration lapse earlier and it's harder to maintain everyone's focus. If you have a lot to cover, you need to break it up into smaller chunks, and find ways to make it as lean as possible.

THE THREE SWEET SPOT GOALS OF WORKSHOPPING THE VALUE OF UX

1. Create greater transparency and team alignment

In going through the process of workshopping something together, you are building greater shared empathy towards your users; and for you, a greater understanding of the business goals and your co-workers' mindsets and motivations.

2. Generate buy-in of your design process

Co-designing gives your co-workers, stakeholders and clients a tangible stake in the outcome, resulting in greater value to them and therefore greater buy-in of the UX process. This can often result in others selling the value of UX on your behalf.

3. Add credibility and support for future UX work

Socialising your workshop outcomes will help stakeholders or clients better understand the value of UX. This helps build extra credibility in your UX practice and, over time, reduces the number of obstacles you'll face. That means less 'defending' and more 'designing' for you.

Remote workshop tools

I am often asked, "What are the best tools for remote workshops?" The answer to this is really: It depends. You need to find the right tool that works for your organisation. If your business uses Google G-Suite for example, then you are likely to use Google Hangouts. G-Suite has a number of excellent collaboration tools that I use. And there are plenty of other options with Microsoft Office 365. (I'm sure after I write this, there will be a whole load more tools that come on the market that will make remote workshopping even easier.) As with UX design, it's not learning the tool itself that with elevate you as a UX leader, it is all the other soft skills I have covered in this book around communication, empathy, mindset and a willingness to adapt and experiment until you find that sweet spot between your users and your business.

As a Google user, when facilitating a remote design workshop which requires sketching, I recommend Google's Jam tool. You can use it with a dedicated Google Jam board if your business has one, but even an iPad and Apple pencil, or a decent Wacom tablet will work well too. If you are doing any type of card sorting (like in my principles workshop mentioned below), you can use Google Draw, where you can set up all your cards and allow direct collaboration with your participants on the drawing canvas in real time.

Failing that, use whatever your team already knows how to use. Even if it's your laptop camera pointed at a whiteboard — that's a start.

The value of UX design principles

UX principles are a great help to communicate the rationale behind your design but it's difficult to simply create a set of principles and get them approved. If the person you are seeking approval from doesn't fully understand the purpose or was not involved in the process, they are unlikely to approve anything. So, when facilitating any co-creating activities or workshops with your team, include the decision makers also. By incorporating their thoughts and feelings about the product and taking on-board the business goals and vision, you should get better support and buy-in.

A UX principles workshop is a great way to build a shared understanding between you, your co-workers and the stakeholders. You can then ease them into the mindset of envisioning the product from the perspective of the customer. You can start with your immediate team — your business analysts, developers, other designers — these people will become your allies and help support decisions in alignment with your shared principles.

In my next book, I have included details of a collaborative principles workshop which I developed over the years. It is primarily geared around direct alignment between designers and product teams and how to effectively communicate the value of UX design to extended teams of non-designers, such as stakeholders and senior managers.

'RULE OF THUMB' PRINCIPLES

TIP: Get your co-workers familiar with some 'rule of thumb' principles before you begin workshopping your own bespoke UX principles. For example, you can start with Jakob Nielsen's heuristic interaction design principles.[16]

THE ART OF PRESENTING

Deductive presentation method

In the real world of UX in business, you have to adapt your presentation to suit your different audience types, including the time-poor execs in the room (and those who think they are). Often, UX designers use what's called a *deductive* method to present findings. This means giving a thesis statement up front and then supporting that statement with multiple points, or evidence.

This method is great for your immediate team, where you already have their trust and support. For example, a presentation showing the results of a recent user testing study might start with the problem you were trying to solve, the design you used, who you tested it with, what you uncovered (including your evidence) and then showing your design recommendations or wireframe specifications. You might then conclude by suggesting next steps such as doing further testing or proceed to detailed designs.

Often this is fine, particularly if your audience is quite technical or analytical and want the design details. I often do this type of presentation to members of my own product team who already trust me. But the problem I have found over the years is that while this presentation format can fly with some people, for others it causes conflict and debate, particularly time-poor stakeholders.

Why?

- Executives are impatient and want you to get straight to the point without dragging them through all your design solutions and

---

[16] https://www.nngroup.com/articles/ten-usability-heuristics/

evidence. Often with the deductive method, you present several pages of solutions with explanations to support your original claim, and then get into micro-discussions about specific design features.

- Difficult stakeholders like to challenge you and presenting things in this format is like presenting an argument primed to be challenged. Even though you have evidence, like a court case, your opposition will challenge your evidence and then you can end up in endless circles of debate, pulling in witnesses (your user videos) to support your argument.

So, if you struggle with stakeholders such as senior managers, you should also be prepared to change your presentation utilising an *inductive* method, which should be your go-to format for busy people. Use this approach when presenting to stakeholders, execs and other time-poor businesspeople.

Inductive presentation method

The inductive method is like telling a series of inspiring stories to allow your audience to draw their own conclusions. You are thus disempowered from asking for their permission and place the responsibility to make the right decision in the hands of your audience.

Every story has a structure — a beginning, a middle and an end — and incorporates a hero's journey (as mentioned earlier). You take your audience on a journey that articulates the ordinary world at the start of the story (the current state), an inspiring call to adventure (the problem to solve), followed by the obstacles needed to overcome (the design challenges or issues faced), which leads back to the better world (the desired future state).

Example:

A. The master vision or 'theme'
Write this like a trailer of a movie, so you don't need to read all the content to understand what the story is about. This section is what I normally shape into an elevator pitch suitable for senior executives. Consider a statement or metaphor to refer to throughout the presentation. It could be a key mantra or design principle that the business has set, for example, "Saving time and effort".

B. The current state
This is usually the 'undesirable past' but doesn't always have to be negative. You could provide a background of some of the great work done to date, highlighting some high-level metrics that support progress in the overall journey to increase user satisfaction.

C. The problem to solve
Clearly articulate the problem to solve, and one or two key issues uncovered in the last round of testing. Refer to your theme or master vision. For example, "We know we want to save our customers time and effort, so doing these things is important."

D. The desired future state
Give an example of the future, such as, "Saving time and effort for customers creates a better user experience and will likely have a direct impact on uptake of the widget, and therefore increase sales and revenue, which we can easily measure the success of."

Set the call to action: Ask for their expert opinion on your design ideas, directing the discussion towards choice rather than debate:

1. Propose option x
2. Propose option y
3. Propose option z

Appendix: The evidence
This is the appropriate time to show all your detailed stats and evidence for those who want to delve deeper.

Deductive vs inductive

The format of the presentation is an important aspect of its storytelling. Without realising it, UX designers often use the *deductive* method to present findings. This means giving a thesis statement up-front then supporting that statement with multiple points or evidence. It's the go-to format mainly because it follows a logical process of giving a proposed reason with specific instances afterwards that support it. While I do use this, I tend to use an *inductive* format more frequently as it appeals to a wider audience.

Inductive is really just about better storytelling

Inductive might sound like a fancy term, but to me it's really just about better story telling. Rather than writing a research paper full of scientific evidence (big yawn for a lot of executives), present them with a story that captures and inspires them, and creates more trust in you. You want to leave them with confidence in your (collaborative) approach, and that you are working hard to improve the user experience because it will help achieve their business goals.

A good executive leader should empower their staff with trust to do a good job, not micromanage them to death by making them validate every decision. That's why in an inductive format, I try to present specific instances of user research or evidence intertwined with some motivational factors to inspire trust and leads to a forgone conclusion.

THE ART OF STORYTELLING

The difference between failure and success

Storytelling is so important in the art of communicating the value of UX to stakeholders and clients. Why? Well, if you consider a failed presentation: one that didn't resonate with the audience; an audience who was disengaged, on their phones, or undermining your presentation by interrupting with irrelevant points, or starting side-conversations with colleagues; then you can see that a poorly executed story could be the difference between failure and success in presenting UX.

We've all experienced it at some point — that feeling of frustration and embarrassment when things don't turn out as expected. In a worst-case scenario, a poorly presented concept can end up going nowhere whilst other less-compelling ideas get developed.

But the good news is, if you work in UX you'll realise you are working in a gold mine of storytelling material — we have such great stories to tell from speaking to our customers, and the data to support our findings. Sure, these alone still won't motivate the most demanding audience, but if the story itself is crafted well you will definitely start to see an improvement in the success in your UX presentations.

An idea communicated badly

A bad presentation of your design is where heated debates begin. Where defending design decisions start, and where the see-saw of "uselessly agreeable" vs "a jerk no one can work with" starts its endless action.

The art of storytelling is clearly critical, and actually quite simple when you understand the basic method of presenting for business. It is about articulating your design in the right way to the right people. A lot of UX designers start off by trying to prove something, almost expecting a conflict, and position their presentation to pre-emptively defend their design. In this scenario, they focus purely on the results or the evidence of what they've gleaned, which in fact often translates into a negative. The premise of this type of presentation is to say to your audience, "I've designed something I think is good, here's the evidence to prove why I think it's good. Challenge me."

If your presentations usually follow this format, then you have been opening up your work as an opportunity for debate. You are asking your audience to challenge your expert opinion, and their responses can often seem more obstructive than constructive: "I wouldn't have done it that way"; "It's not what my customers want"; "I could have told you that without any testing "; or "You only tested it with five people — what would the sixth person say?"

A better way to approach a presentation is to spend the time crafting it into a story. It can take a bit of practice, but the results usually speak for themselves. You know your design is sound, and you have the evidence from users to prove you are on the right path, so the objective is not to prove it, but to get your audience inside your head, and inside the head of the customer. First, you want to get them on-board with the problem, and then compare it to a new world in which your design helps to make it a better place. In this scenario, you never say you have all of the answers, or that you have solved all the problems, rather you frame your story as your contribution to improving the customer's world, whilst also addressing the needs of the business.

For me, the realisation of the true power of storytelling has been a culmination of a lot of trial and error over the years, and you may find the same is true for you also. The reason is that a story that resonates has a lot to do with the type of audience you are speaking to.

USING VIDEO TO TELL A STORY

Remember that a presentation doesn't have to be a static PowerPoint presentation. In fact, too many dull slides could easily undo your hard work in telling an engaging story.

TIP: Consider utilising your design skills to convert key parts (or all) of your presentation into a compelling video story. This is likely to make it more engaging than a speaker-led slideshow alone and storyboarding a video sequence can actually help formulate a compelling theme for your presentation.

Finding the right 'shape' for your story

There is a great Ted Talk called "The Secret Structure of Great Talks" by Nancy Duarte.[17] She sums up the process of articulating the current state vs the desired future state brilliantly, and this is a great format to use as it works well for lots of things.

When shaping the story for your master vision or theme, you want to start by capturing your audience's imagination and inspire them to act later. Pick something that resonates with execs. For example, at the 2019 CX Summit[18] in Sydney, Kristin Embury, Vice President of Global Customer Service at Netflix, told us their call centre goal was to get customers back to streaming. This mantra was used to inspire call-centre staff to resolve issues quickly to reduce friction for customers. Getting them back to streaming quicker had an impact on the bottom-line of customer satisfaction.

When highlighting your current state (A.K.A. the status quo) try to add in some high-level numbers or stats for added effect. Referring to industry insights or your own data if you have some can prove to be useful in articu-

---

[17] https://www.ted.com/talks/nancy_duarte_the_secret_structure_of_great_talks
[18] Embury, K. (2019, 30 October). *How to build, organise & run a leading customer service team* [Conference presentation]. Customer Experience Summit, Sydney, NSW, Australia. https://forefrontevents.com.au/wp-content/uploads/2019/08/CX-Summit-NSW.pdf

lating the undesirable past. But don't overdo it — you just want to highlight the status quo, and lead into the problem to solve.

CURRENT STATE VS FUTURE STATE

TIP: The current state doesn't have to be the current state of your own product (although it's likely to be a focus somewhere in this); it could also be a reference to your competitors.

The desired future state doesn't have to be your design solution. It could be someone else's. You could highlight how Uber revolutionised the cab-ride industry, or how Otter helped organisations reduce friction with effortless note-taking in meetings.

When presenting your problem to solve, frame it as a roadblock in the vision or goal; the challenge/s to overcome in order to move away from the status quo. You could include a few verbatim statements or videos of problems captured from real customers to help articulate the problem. Again, don't overdo it as you can point to detailed evidence later if asked. When presenting your future state recommendations, you want it to come across as a lightbulb moment revealing the desired future state with the problem removed, as compared to the undesirable past. As Duarte suggests in her Ted Talk, you can go back and forth, traversing between what is and what could be. The intent here is to make your desired future state always more appealing and draw them into what could be a better world for the customer.

Conclude by inspiring them to act, creating an "Ah-ha" moment where you show how your vision relates back to the theme, hinting at a call-to-action that inspires your audience to want to act to help create a better world. You've done your bit to move forward towards the new bliss in your story; now the future is in their hands. For example, you can demonstrate how your idea helps remove friction, leading to increased customer satisfaction, taking them one step closer to the ideal future state of your theme or mantra, or principle of "saving our customers time and effort".

You could also include a quote from a customer commenting on something they liked, or a comment they had about what this future state might be like for them, and how it would change their world. This is not evidence, just part of your story.

SHOWING YOUR EVIDENCE (THE CREDITS)

After the story concludes, and your audience is pleading for an encore, this is the time where you can delve into all your evidence. If your presentation was a movie, this would be your credit roll — the data and details of how you did it that way and why. It's there for the benefit of those who want to delve deeper and understand in more detail how you propose to solve the problem.

CREATING YOUR ELEVATOR PITCH

Consider how your opening slide or sequence to your presentation comes across to senior executives. It's best to capture your vision in a short and succinct statement of intent for your work, and clearly articulate the value that it delivers to them. There is a great guide and template to help you formulate your elevator pitch on the Atlassian website.[19]

---

[19] www.atlassian.com/team-playbook

CHAPTER SEVEN

I've given you an awful lot to consider, haven't I? Taking your business on the journey, becoming a good facilitator, speaking the right language, and defending design decisions without defending decisions. That's why I have structured the final chapter of this book as a simple series of seven steps you can follow to improve your UX communication techniques within your organisation. Be sure to refer to the previous chapters for more detail as needed.

"The acquisition of skills requires a regular environment, an adequate opportunity to practice, and rapid and unequivocal feedback about the correctness of thoughts and actions."

– Daniel Kahneman [20]

In order to become more successful and to gain more leverage for your UX practice, you need to do the following:

STEP 1.
UNDERSTAND WHO YOU ARE TALKING TO

To be a successful UX designer and gain more leverage for your practice, you should adopt a style of language that your business can relate to. Practice the art of communication with your co-workers and extended team members within your organisation.

One of the many challenges we all face as UX designers is that the business we work for often doesn't understand UX, or how to apply it into their existing ways of working. It's no wonder then that a UX designer can feel their work is often misunderstood or the business they work for is misinformed.

---

[20] Kahneman, D. (2012). *Thinking, fast and slow.* [ePub]. Penguin Books.

Conducting stakeholder interviews or 'safaris' and creating some team personas in the same way you would for your customers is a great start. Use these to help tailor your language around the needs of your business and have empathy with the motivations behind what your co-workers and stakeholders or clients are trying to achieve as their primary goal.

Things to do:
- Refine your communication style
- Conduct stakeholder safaris
- Create organisational / team personas

STEP 2.
SHIFT YOUR MINDSET FROM A DESIGN IMPLEMENTER TO A DESIGN LEADER

Empathise outwards by fully understanding your users' needs and motivations, but also empathise inwards by treating co-workers and stakeholders like your users. Remember, without your organisation's requirements you would not have a product to work on, nor users. So, empathy for your organisation means understanding your stakeholder's frustrations, goals and expectations of the product.

Lead by example for other members in your team or co-workers; whether they are designers, developers or something else, your mindset should be reinforced by those around you. As a leader, you set the principles in motion, have all the hard conversations with stakeholders, and ensure that educating and evangelising becomes part of your culture.

On top of that you should try to establish a mentor-level leadership. Don't wait for someone to ask you to be their mentor as there are many who want to learn and can benefit from what you have to offer. Mentoring can give others in your team the confidence they need to succeed themselves.

Things to do:
- Seek a mentor
- Become a mentor
- Attend guest speaking events and communicate learnings to others
- Evangelise your UX vision to stakeholders

STEP 3.
CONDUCT SOME COMPELLING UX RESEARCH, WHATEVER IT IS, AND HIGHLIGHT IT OFTEN

You should always look for the opportunity to arm yourself with data. Make it your job to seek out user stats and information that will help educate your colleagues about your users. Back your designs with evidence from direct customer research and user videos (your research) or indirect customer research (other people's research such as articles, white papers or competitor reviews). When asked to deliver a solution or feature that is lacking in proper user research, make sure you deliver some user context. Whilst many UX designers would like to always do full user testing, that's not always feasible. But you can always do something — whether it is guerrilla testing in a café or corridor testing to highlight a key concern, or dissecting user feedback from your app or website into a compelling customer journey — the aim is to provide a clear user perspective at the start of any new piece of UX work to encourage making the right decisions, not just following business goals and objectives.

There are many other types of valid research that you can do, like desk research (e.g. studying someone else's research journals, or finding out more about the business goals and vision), talking to your data expert about analytics, or delving into them yourself, and have discussions with key SMEs such as call centre operatives.

Use these findings as 'insights for investigation' or 'problems uncovered' that you can use in your presentations to help promote the need of doing more UX work.

Things to do:
- Primary or desk research
- SME interviews or discussions
- Guerrilla or corridor testing
- Data / visual analytics reviews
- Showcase it in a Wiki page, on a wall, and via roadshow presentations

STEP 4.
MASTER THE ART OF UX COMMUNICATION FOR BEST RESULTS

Working with people can be hard work. On your journey to becoming a UX leader, you will encounter all types of people, and work across all types of team cultures and environments. Not everyone in every team will get along. If you are starting out in UX, navigating this business-human landscape can be hard going; there will be clashing viewpoints and personalities, pressing deadlines leading to rash decisions, and debates about what should and shouldn't be built.

To navigate this demanding landscape, developing and maintaining the right mindset is crucial. I know a lot of designers who have been afraid to speak their minds (we are all sensitive at heart) but gaining the confidence to speak your mind is important. Also important is the art of listening to feedback without taking it personally. Cultivating confidence in a challenging environment can be hard, but the first step is to listen and empathise.

Things to do:
- Learn the art of effective UX communication as outlined in this book
- Extend your reading list to incorporate books that cover business mindset

Like anything, practise makes perfect. You may not nail every technique in this book straight away, but if you start small you can iterate and improve over time. Constantly refining your UX communication style, as outlined in this book, will help you become a better strategic leader and take the business you work for on the journey of what UX is, and why it matters to them and to their customers.

STEP 5.
ALIGN YOUR UX WORK WITH YOUR BUSINESS THROUGH CO-DESIGN WORKSHOPS

Master the art of workshopping to guide team members and stakeholders through your UX design process. Just taking the time to design together is extremely beneficial and you can start small and build up over time. A simple workshop with a few colleagues is all you need — anything that is designed to help your co-workers or business teams to become more aligned around your UX practice, and help you become better at applying your craft within your organisation.

Things to do:

- Conduct co-designed workshops (as often as you can)
- Conduct a proto-personas workshop
- Conduct a UX vision workshop
- Conduct a UX principles workshop

Each of the above will be covered in more detail in my next book

STEP 6.
CONTINUALLY PROVE THE VALUE OF YOUR UX ACTIVITIES

Be sure to incorporate some UX metrics wherever possible. There are some great methods online that are well documented: SEQ, SUS, SUPR-Q, Google Heart, and more. Find something that works for what you are doing and be sure to get input from any data enthusiasts, such as a conversion optimisation specialist or anyone who has extensive expertise in data analytics.

Ideally, you should aim to work with stakeholders to create a UX dashboard that will help establish UX rigor to highlight the success of the work you are doing, including full journey metrics, customer feedback, and any other supporting research that is of value to your organisation.

Things to do:

- Competitor / market review
- Bring the 'good news' numbers or user comments to your meetings
- Conduct user testing scores
- Create a UX dashboard

STEP 7.
START EVANGELISING UPWARDS AND DOWNWARDS

Use great storytelling to evangelise upwards and downwards by sharing both your users' frustrations and expectations, and opportunities for success, to your team and to your business in a way they understand and can relate to.

Start by conducting a "What is UX" roadshow or add slides to your existing presentations that tackle some of the common misconceptions about what UX is and isn't. Use this as a tool to promote your process, showcase some of the key methods you use, back it up with case studies and results, and be sure to explain how the role of UX is beneficial to the bottom-line of the business.

Leverage the art of storytelling to make it compelling and interesting, inciting people to want to be involved and back you up.

Things to do:
- Conduct a "What is UX" roadshow
- Showcase case studies with success metrics
- Gather and highlight compelling customer feedback

Each of the above will be covered in more detail in my next book

WHAT NEXT?

I hope you have enjoyed this book. The focus of this publication has been on the art of effective communication and mindset and overcoming UX challenges in the business landscape.

My next book, "Sweet Spot UX Workshops: Effective Design Facilitation for Perfect Business Alignment" will focus on some of the practical workshops mentioned earlier that will help you articulate your UX practices more effectively, and help you align and build your UX capability within the business where you work.

The practical workshops covered in my next book are:
- Design workshop basics
- Proto-personas workshop
- UX vision workshop
- UX principles workshop
- "What is UX" roadshow presentation
- Creating a UX dashboard
- Plus more....

FINAL WORD

DEVELOPING A UX GROWTH MINDSET

The term 'growth mindset' now feels overused, but if there's one key mindset message to take away from this book, it is that mistakes are okay and enable you to grow as a designer. Mistakes are actually just experiments that didn't work as expected — like a design experiment the results, whether positive or negative, always enable you to learn something.

Every organisation is different, and you have to be prepared to adapt based on feedback. To expect the organisation to completely shift around you and your design style or UX methods is too optimistic. As you wouldn't expect your users to adapt their behaviours in order to use your product; the same is true of your business.

In my experience, you will always find that what works in one organisation may not work in another, so success is recognising that your UX practice is its own design experiment — if it doesn't work, try something else. Your role as a UX leader is to take them on the journey; to guide and educate, rather than argue and defend.

If you think about it, as a UX designer, you allow your users to stumble through your product and welcome them to highlight any usability issues so you can learn more about them and improve your product. The same is true for you and your relationship with your organisation. In growing as a UX designer, never dwell on negative feedback — simply treat it like a work in progress, a prototype that's rich in feedback and ever-changing and enables you to gain more understanding.

Owning your shortcomings is also respectable — be open and transparent about what you know and what you don't. Highlight any failures as part of your journey in trying to make the world a better place for your customers, and in trying to understand the goals of the business. Adopting a UX growth mindset is as much about growing as a person as well as a UX designer.

MIKE NEWMAN

STAY CURIOUS

KEEP LEARNING

HAVE EMPATHY

BE CONFIDENT

GOOD LUCK

ABOUT THE AUTHOR

MIKE NEWMAN, UX DESIGN CONSULTANT

Mike Newman is a UX professional with a design background of 20+ years. During this time, he worked on and led many high profile UX design initiatives across a range of industries including banking, retail, telco, media, travel, construction, and government.

Mike started his career as a designer in the early 2000s when web design (as it was known back then) was still in its infancy. He quickly recognised that the real key to getting customers to adopt a new software product was to really understand it from their perspective. Barclays Bank in England was one of the early adopters of user-centred design practices and it was there that Mike began his career in User Experience (UX).

Mike now lives in Sydney, Australia, where he is recognised as an industry expert in customer-first design and where he helps businesses improve their digital products, making them more meaningful to their users.

With his insistence on a collaborative design process and a welcoming approach to mentoring other designers, his goal with this book is to help UX designers master the art of communicating User Experience effectively to their clients and stakeholders.

ACKNOWLEDGEMENTS

I would like to thank everybody who kindly provided feedback and input for this book. In particular, I would like to extend a very special thank you to the following people for their perspectives, support and motivation:

Jack Rex, Slawka Tymosiewicz, Kevin Raccani, Javince Chan, Andrew Akratos, Teresa Goudie, Jane Turner, Kieran Bianca, Tara Hickman, Mum and Dad.

Lightning Source UK Ltd.
Milton Keynes UK
UKHW010403011222
413111UK00012B/2243

9 780645 040434